Revision  Guides

PEARSON
PUBLISHING

D1392283

GCSE English
and English Literature

James Durran and Jim Stewart

James Durran is Head of English at Parkside Community College in Cambridge.
Jim Stewart is Head of English at St Peter's School in Huntingdon.

Cartoons by Steve Clarke

GCSE English and English Literature

Name ....

Class..

School ....

....

Dates of exams:

1 ....

2 ....

3 ....

Exam board ....

Syllabus numbers...

Candidate number..

Centre number ....

Further copies of this publication may be obtained from:

Pearson Publishing
Chesterton Mill, French's Road, Cambridge CB4 3NP
Tel 01223 350555   Fax 01223 356484

Email info@pearson.co.uk   Web site http://www.pearson.co.uk/education/

ISBN: 1 85749 544 6

Published by Pearson Publishing 1999
© Pearson Publishing 1999
Sixth reprint 2000

Contents

Contents

Introduction

*Although she'd never know it,
she was having an existential experience*

This guide is designed to help you to work effectively on your own as you prepare for the NEAB exams in GCSE English and GCSE English Literature. It will not replace the work that you do in school with your English teacher, but it will help you to revise what you have learned during the GCSE course.

It will also help you to structure your revision and make the most efficient use of your time as you prepare for the exams. The activities are designed to help you to feel more confident about tackling the exams. They do this by helping you to see what you already know, and showing you how to make the best use of this knowledge.

What advice does the guide give?

The guide gives advice on:

◆ what the examiners are looking for

◆ revising and preparing for each section of the exams

◆ annotating your exam texts effectively

◆ practising planning and writing exam answers

◆ reading exam papers and understanding exactly what the questions are asking for

◆ planning and organising your time in the exams

◆ quoting effectively

◆ effective use of technical terms

◆ developing reading skills.

The guide starts with general advice, and there is then a separate section on each part of the English and English Literature exams.

There is also a guide to technical terms that you may find useful (see *Chapter 8*).

How can you use the guide?

 The guide suggests activities that will help you to revise and prepare for the exam. These are shown by this icon.

Some of the activities do not ask you to write much at all – just to think, to mark texts and, perhaps, make a few notes. These will give you confidence that you do have things to write.

Some suggest very short pieces of writing, which will help you to write quickly and concisely, putting complicated ideas into a few words. This is a very important skill in the exam.

There are also some suggestions for longer pieces of writing to do – very useful if you have the time.

Many of the activities in the guide would also be suitable for you to work on with a friend, or in a group of friends. The discussion involved in sorting out your ideas will be very helpful. However, you should practise writing on your own, too.

Some of the activities are divided into easy, less easy and hard. You might want to start with the easy activities, and work your way through, or you may decide to start with the less easy or hard activities. You might want to ask your teacher to suggest which activities are best for you. The activities are shown by these icons:

 Easy   **Less easy**   **Hard**

The exam papers

NEAB English Paper 1

Section A: Reading non-fiction materials
You will have to read and answer questions on some texts that you have not seen before (see *Chapter 2*, page 9).

Section B: Writing to argue, persuade or instruct
You will have to do a piece of writing which may be connected to the texts in Section A (see *Chapter 3*, page 21).

NEAB English Paper 2

Section A:
Part 1 One of the poets in the NEAB *Anthology*
You will have to write for half an hour about the poems by one poet that you have studied (see *Chapter 5*, page 42).

Part 2 'Poems from other cultures and traditions' in the NEAB *Anthology*
You will have to write for half an hour about the poems that you have studied (see *Chapter 5*, page 42).

Section B: Writing to inform, explain or describe
You will have to do a piece of writing, which may be connected to the poems in Section A (see *Chapter 4*, page 32).

NEAB English Literature

Section A: Prose text
You will have to write for an hour about the novel or the short stories that you have studied (see *Chapters 6 and 7*, pages 58 and 74).

Section B: 'Pre-twentieth and twentieth century poetry', from the NEAB *Anthology*
You will have to write for an hour about the group, or groups, of poems that you have studied (see *Chapter 5*, page 42).

1 General advice

The main sections of this chapter are:

◆ Looking back over your GCSE work

◆ Practising planning and writing

◆ The exam papers

◆ Reading exam questions

◆ Quoting

Looking back over your GCSE work

Spend some time getting all your notes and other work into order, if you have not already done so.

Look back over the pieces of writing that you have done during the course, especially:

◆ Year 10 and 11 assignments

◆ exam practices

◆ mock exam answers.

He did not recall a single worksheet, but he recognised the gum

Look at how your writing has developed.
Look at the comments from your teacher.

You could make some quick notes on the following things:

◆ **Working in exam conditions** – What have you learned about what you need to improve in this? For example, do you read the questions carefully? Do you plan effectively? Do you spend the right amount of time on each question? There is lots of advice on this later in the guide.

◆ **Aspects of your writing** – What do you need to improve about the way that you write in exams? This includes all writing – about the *Anthology*, unseen texts, literature texts, and different kinds of original writing.

◆ **Technical accuracy** – Marks are given – and lost – in the exam for technical accuracy (spelling and punctuation) and presentation (including handwriting). What, exactly, do **you** need to improve?

Practising planning and writing

Planning

One very effective way of revising is to practise planning exam answers. Your teacher will give you sample questions to work on.

The plan you write might take the form of a flow diagram, showing the order of the points you will make. It might be a quick note of events to refer to, or pages of a novel to find quotations on. It might be a spider diagram, showing which examples or points you will refer to in each section of your essay. If you practise, you will find a method that works for you. This is an example of a useful, quick plan for an answer about symbolic objects in *Lord of the Flies*:

When practising, you could spend a long time planning carefully and thinking hard about what to include in your essay. However, you could just give yourself a few minutes, as though you are in the actual exam. That way, you can do several practice plans in a short time.

Writing

Practising writing parts of answers, or whole answers, is very valuable. You might even persuade your teacher to mark one or two.

In Lord of the Flies, the most impo symbolic. The fire. All of th and the uses, but also practical character Piggy, for example times in the or at th later. The

◆ It is useful to practise writing just the beginnings of answers. Start with a quick plan and then write just the opening paragraph. You could take your time over this, thinking through how to make your opening as effective as possible. Alternatively, give yourself five minutes to practise writing under pressure.

◆ It is also very useful to practise whole timed answers: your teacher will give you some examples of questions. Give yourself exactly the amount of time you would have in the exam. Check that you know what this is. (It won't be more than an hour.) Start by making a quick plan or use one of the opening paragraphs that you have written.

"Could you just mark these... ?"

◆ As you are revising, try putting key ideas into words. For example, you might have an idea about a character, or an idea about what a writer is saying: experiment with expressing this idea in one short paragraph. Could you put it more clearly? Could you weave in a quotation?

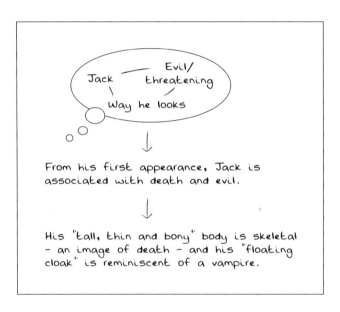

From his first appearance, Jack is associated with death and evil.

His "tall, thin and bony" body is skeletal – an image of death – and his "floating cloak" is reminiscent of a vampire.

◆ Pick out an important phrase or sentence from a text you are revising. Try writing a sentence or two to explain the significance of this quotation: again, experiment with ways to make your explanation as clear as possible. Look at how this has been done in the example above.

The exam papers

To be well prepared, you need to know certain facts about the papers before you go into the exam room. These will include:

- how long each paper lasts

- how long you are expected to spend on each question

- what type of questions to expect on each paper and in each section (some are worth more marks than others)

- what particular skills each question is asking you to use

- whether you will need to write anything in rough and how long you should spend doing this

- what prepared texts you will be writing about and in which questions.

"But I hardly know you..."

Reading exam questions

The most important part of being successful in an exam is what might seem to be the simplest – answering what the question is asking. It is possible in the stress of exam conditions to misread or misunderstand the questions, but, with care, you can avoid this altogether.

Chapter 9 contains sample questions, annotated with advice and explanations of key words. Look through them carefully – but remember that the questions may not be exactly like these, as the way they are presented can change from year to year.

*As he raced to finish his second essay, he spotted the word **or**…*

Many of the questions have bullet points, which are designed to help you think more deeply about what the question is asking for.

They also break the question down into smaller parts, to help you to structure your answer.

Read the advice about bullet points in *Chapter 8*.

Quoting

Using quotations well is a very effective way of improving your grades. It is important that you are confident about doing this.

There is advice in each chapter about making the best use of quotations for each section of the exam papers.

2 Reading non-fiction texts

In **Section A of English Paper 1**, you will have to read and write about non-fiction texts that you have not seen before. There will probably be at least two texts. These might include newspaper or magazine articles, information leaflets or advertisements, for example.

You will have prepared for and practised this in class. This chapter offers:

◆ advice about how to tackle the exam

◆ some ideas about what you should revise

◆ some suggestions for how you can do some more preparation on your own.

She was beginning to question whether this wasn't a work of fiction after all...

What the examiners are looking for

✔ Can you read texts thoughtfully and critically?

✔ Can you compare different texts and their effects?

✔ Can you tell the difference between fact and opinion?

✔ Can you show understanding of how information has been presented for particular audiences?

✔ Can you follow an argument and point out where it doesn't work?

✔ Can you find information and recognise ideas in a text, especially when they are not stated directly?

✔ Can you choose suitable examples and quotations from more than one text?

✔ Do you understand how texts are structured and presented to create particular effects?

Tackling the exam paper

Reading the paper

This section tests your skills as a reader. When you open the paper you will find two or three non-fiction texts, which you will have to read and answer questions on. These may be on separate sheets.

It is very important that you read the questions before you read the texts. It would be a waste of time to read the texts first: you should be looking for particular ideas, features and information while you read.

Your first reading of the texts should be detailed. Use a pen, pencil or highlighter to mark useful points. You might:

◆ put a line in the margin next to a significant paragraph or sentence

◆ underline important phrases, or circle key words

◆ write words and phrases in the margin.

As you read, keep an eye on the questions. What do you need to look for?

For example:

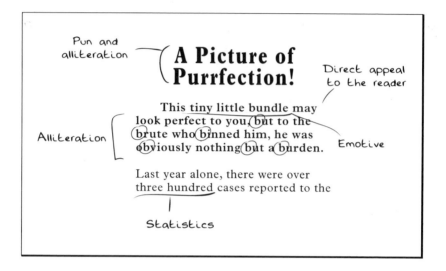

In *Chapter 9*, there are examples of questions, together with advice.

Timing

This section will be divided into several questions. It is very important that you look at how many marks there are for each. You should spend the most time, and write the most, on the question worth the highest number of marks.

Fact and opinion

The first, shorter questions will probably ask you to find particular information or ideas in the texts. To do this you will have to know the difference between fact and opinion.

Even if you are asked to list points, you should put these in your own words as far as possible. To show that you understand what you have found, you may need to explain it.

Planning

For the longer questions, the examiners will be looking for evidence that you have put your ideas into order before starting to write. Make a quick list of points or a diagram of your ideas: don't just launch into the writing. For example, if you are comparing two texts, you might quickly make two lists – of similarities and of differences.

Referring back to the texts

You will, of course, have to look back at the texts as you write your answers – to find information and examples, and to choose words and phrases to quote. You will not have time to reread the texts word for word. Your markings will help, but you will need to skim and scan the text, looking for key words and topics.

This kind of reading is not about reading individual words, one after the other. It is about looking at large chunks of text, and spotting particular words or ideas in them. You need to get used to looking at a whole page at a time. This involves moving your eye quickly down the page, stopping at three or four points, and looking for key words or phrases.

 Practise this with a magazine or newspaper article. Read it once, then skim through it quickly looking for all the references to a particular person, place, or idea.

Checking and correcting

Leave yourself time to check your answers at the end. Five minutes should be enough.

Checklists of ideas

The lists below are all ideas that you should be familiar with. You will need them when you are answering questions on the texts, writing about how effective they are, and especially when you are comparing texts with each other. Tick the ones you are confident about:

Language

- [ ] assertion
- [ ] audience
- [ ] caption
- [ ] emotive language
- [ ] fact
- [ ] headline
- [ ] narrative
- [ ] opinion
- [ ] persuasive language
- [ ] puns
- [ ] register
- [ ] repetition
- [ ] rhetorical questions
- [ ] sentence lengths
- [ ] slogan
- [ ] stereotype
- [ ] structure
- [ ] tone
- [ ] voice

Presentation

- [ ] bullet points
- [ ] caption
- [ ] headline
- [ ] layout
- [ ] logo
- [ ] pictures
- [ ] slogan

You will find explanations of all these terms in *Chapter 8*.

There are lots of other features of language, that you are used to finding in poetry and stories but which might be in these texts as well. For example, imagery, metaphor, simile, alliteration, personification, onomatopoeia, symbolism, and so on. You will find explanations of all these in *Chapter 8*, too.

Comparing texts

On this paper you will be asked to compare two or more texts, and the question that asks you to do this will carry more marks than any of the others. The bullet points in the question will help. Make sure that you cover each one. You should be writing about how the texts are similar and how they are different in the following ways:

◆ What are the writers trying to do?

◆ How are the texts aimed at particular readers?

◆ How have the writers used language?

◆ How is each text presented on the page?

◆ How are the texts structured differently from each other?

◆ What is the tone of each text?

◆ How effective is each text?

◆ What is your response to each text and which do you prefer?

(See section on *Planning*, on page 13.)

Quoting

When you are writing about the non-fiction texts in the exam, it is very important that you quote from the text. Well-chosen quotations show your understanding of the text and of the point that you are making.

For example:

> Whereas the leaflet presents facts, the newspaper article tries to persuade the reader to agree with the writer's point of view, and this is reflected in the language of both. The leaflet refers neutrally to "the new GCSE", whereas the article refers emotively to "the dreaded new exam at 16".

"A rose by any other name..."

Practising planning and writing

One of the most effective ways to revise for this part of the exam is to get used to tackling the kinds of questions that are in the paper. Your teacher will give you examples of these to practise with. Look at the advice on *Practising planning and writing* in *Chapter 1*.

Leaflet	Newspaper article
More factual	More opinion
Neutral tone	Angry tone
More formal	More informal
Neutral language	Emotive language
More statistics	Statistics selected to support opinions
Informative graphics	Emotive pictures
Layout important	Shorter sentences and paragraphs
Satisfyingly impartial	Obviously biased

Other ways to prepare for this section

For some of the following activities, you will need some non-fiction texts to work with. You could use articles and reports from newspapers and magazines, information leaflets, advertisements, school brochures for parents, Internet pages, CD-ROM pages, campaign leaflets, holiday brochures, etc.

His preparation had bin excellent

 Every time you read a newspaper, magazine, leaflet or advertisement, think about who it is aimed at, and how it has been written with that audience in mind. Look at the language that is being used.

• • • • •

 Collect some of these non-fiction texts. Divide them into ones which are mainly about getting information across, and ones which try to persuade the reader to do or think something. Then look again at the information texts. Can you find anything in them which is, in fact, meant to be persuasive?

Choose a text which has an argument in it – an attempt to persuade the reader to think or feel in the same way as the writer. Go through it and underline what you think are the four main points that the writer is making. You could then try summarising the argument in your own writing, in no more than 50 words.

• • • • •

 Take two or three texts of different kinds. Try to find just one example of each of the things in the following list:

◆ bullet points

◆ emotive language

◆ fact

◆ effective or unusual layout

◆ opinion

◆ persuasive language

◆ repetition, used for effect

◆ a rhetorical question

◆ a slogan

◆ a stereotype

◆ a picture intended to play on the reader's emotions

◆ a clear voice coming through the text

◆ short sentences, used for effect

• • • • •

 Look for two different texts about the same thing. For example, they might be two different newspaper reports on the same event, or a magazine article and a newspaper report on the same topic.

Make a list of similarities and differences between the two texts. You could use this checklist to help you:

☐ What are the writers trying to do?

☐ How are the texts aimed at particular readers?

☐ How have the writers used language?

☐ How is each text presented on the page?

☐ How are the texts structured differently from each other?

☐ What is the tone of each text?

☐ How effective is each text?

☐ What is your response to each text and which do you prefer?

• • • • •

 Find a persuasive or argumentative text. Try to find three facts. Then try to find three opinions. Can you find an opinion that is presented as though it was a fact?

• • • • •

 With the same or a different text, go through and highlight all the emotive words. What is their overall effect?

"Read it to me one last time before I go ..."

3 Writing to argue, persuade or instruct

In **Section B of English Paper 1**, you will have to produce a piece of writing, which will be related to what you have been reading and writing about in Section A of the same paper. There will be three tasks, from which you will have to choose one. This will involve arguing, persuading or instructing, or a mixture of these.

Arguing

means expressing a point of view as clearly and effectively as possible. It will usually involve presenting evidence and a series of reasons.

Persuading

means getting your readers to agree with a point of view or to feel something. It might involve argument, but it will usually also involve other methods of trying to affect people's feelings about something.

Instructing

means explaining how to do something as clearly as possible.

You will have prepared for and practised this in class. This chapter does not attempt to teach you how to do these kinds of writing, but it does offer:

♦ advice about how to tackle the exam

♦ some ideas about what you should revise

♦ some suggestions for how you can do some more preparation on your own.

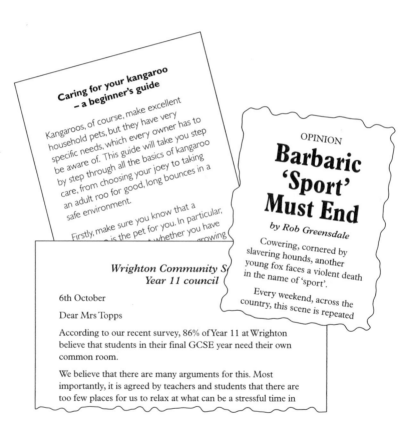

Caring for your kangaroo
– a beginner's guide

Kangaroos, of course, make excellent household pets, but they have very specific needs, which every owner has to be aware of. This guide will take you step by step through all the basics of kangaroo care, from choosing your joey to taking an adult roo for good, long bounces in a safe environment.

Firstly, make sure you know that a ... is the pet for you. In particular, ... whether you have ... growing ...

OPINION

Barbaric 'Sport' Must End

by Rob Greensdale

Cowering, cornered by slavering hounds, another young fox faces a violent death in the name of 'sport'.

Every weekend, across the country, this scene is repeated

Wrighton Community S...
Year 11 council

6th October

Dear Mrs Topps

According to our recent survey, 86% of Year 11 at Wrighton believe that students in their final GCSE year need their own common room.

We believe that there are many arguments for this. Most importantly, it is agreed by teachers and students that there are too few places for us to relax at what can be a stressful time in

What the examiners are looking for

✔ Can you communicate clearly in writing?

✔ Can you write for a particular audience?

✔ Can you use particular forms effectively?

✔ Can you use a wide vocabulary?

✔ Can you organise ideas into sentences, paragraphs and whole texts?

✔ How well can you spell?

 ✔ Can you punctuate accurately?

✔ Can you use standard English when appropriate?

✔ Can you present work neatly and clearly?

✔ How clear and readable is your handwriting?

Unfortunately, her vocabulary was now so wide she couldn't get it through the exam room door...

Tackling the exam paper

Reading the paper

It is very important that you read all of the questions carefully before deciding which to answer. You need to think about the type, or types, of writing that each question asks for, and decide which one you can do best. For example, you may have a choice of writing a magazine article, a letter, or a set of instructions. By now, you should know which type of writing will give you the chance to do your best work – and this will almost certainly be the one to choose.

In *Chapter 9*, there are examples of questions, together with advice.

Planning and writing

You will be given advice at the beginning of Section B about how to spend the hour that is allowed for the question. This will probably suggest that you spend ten minutes planning, 40 minutes writing and then ten minutes checking and correcting what you have written. It is very important that you follow this advice about time.

The examiners will be looking for evidence that you have put your ideas into order before starting to write. Make a list of points or a diagram of your ideas. Careful planning is essential: don't just launch into the writing. Look at the example on page 26.

It is vital that you think very carefully about the purpose and the audience of the piece of writing. The examiners will be looking for evidence that you have done this.

Make sure that you write enough. Often, people lose marks on this section by writing too little. For example, a letter less than a side long is not enough for an hour's writing: you should aim for about two sides.

Presentation

If you are writing a letter, a leaflet or a feature for a magazine, then the way it is laid out or presented will matter. However, you should not spend too long on this: the words are the most important thing.

Make sure that you revise how to set out formal and informal letters.

Checking and correcting

Remember that this is one of the sections in the exam where you can gain or lose marks for spelling, punctuation, grammar and presentation.

Leave yourself time to check your answers at the end. Five minutes should be enough. For example:

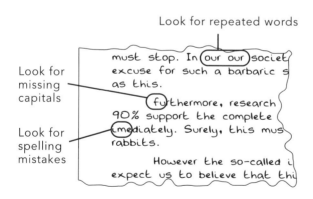

Look for repeated words

Look for missing capitals

Look for spelling mistakes

must stop. In our our society
excuse for such a barbaric s
as this.
        furthermore, research
90% support the complete
mediately. Surely, this mus
rabbits.
        However the so-called i
expect us to believe that thi

Practising planning and writing

Practising the kinds of questions that are in the paper is one of the most effective ways to prepare for this part of the exam. Ask your teacher for examples to work on. Remember to check the advice on *Practising planning and writing* in Chapter 1.

For foxhunting

Tradition
Part of country life
Controls pests
Supports rural economy
Most foxes escape anyway
Hounds would have to be put down if stopped
Tourist attraction
Employment
Arguments against are just sentimental

Against foxhunting

Unnecessary cruelty
Encourages sadism
Better ways exist to control pests
Tradition is no excuse for cruelty
Chase is cruel, even if fox escapes
Not acceptable in modern society

For this section of the exam, it can be particularly useful to practise writing just the beginnings of answers. Look at the examples on page 22.

Other ways to prepare for this section

The preparation that you do for Section A of this paper (thinking about how writers write for particular purposes and audiences) is also important preparation for this section.

She probably wouldn't need it but she had everything else...

Writing an argument

 To practise putting together an argument, make a list of points (in any order) that you would use if you were doing one of the following tasks:

Either

◆ Write a letter to the headteacher of your school, arguing that Year 11 should have their own common room.

Or

◆ Write a speech to deliver to the rest of Year 11, arguing that they should each donate £10 towards buying furniture for the new Year 11 common room.

Now think about the order in which you put these points. Your first and last points will be particularly important. Also, you need to think carefully about the evidence that you will use to support your argument.

The words in the box below are all useful for connecting or starting sentences when you are writing out an argument. Choosing the right words like this can help you to suit your writing to your audience.

Go through the list and pick out one word from each group that would make an argument sound more formal. For example, if you were writing for your headteacher, or trying to sound knowledgeable to the public, you might write "furthermore...", rather than "what's more...". (See **Register** in *Chapter 8*, page 101.)

First(ly)...	Despite this...	It would seem...
Secondly,... (etc)	Alternatively...	In fact...
	On the other hand...	
... because/as...	Whereas...	Clearly...
Consequently...		...of course...
Therefore...	In particular...	Naturally...
Accordingly...	Notably...	Obviously...
Since...	...more important...	Evidently...
Thus...	Significantly...	Surely...
...so...	Specifically...	Certainly...
Hence...	...especially...	
	Above all...	Furthermore...
Equally...		What is more...
Similarly...	For example...	Moreover...
In the same way...	...such as...	In addition...
As with...		
Likewise...	...also...	On the whole...
	...as well as...	To sum up...
However...		Finally...
Although...	...as suggested by...	In conclusion...
Nevertheless...	To show that...	

Now try writing your argument in no more than 200 words. (This is less than you should write in the exam.) As you write, use the words in the list to help you structure your argument, and to help you make it sound convincing.

Writing persuasively

 To practise writing persuasively, try one of the following, in no more than 200 words. (This is less than you should write in the exam.)

Either

◆ Write a leaflet to distribute to the public, putting forward your point of view about a controversial topic, such as drugs, euthanasia, hunting, boxing or gun control.

Or

◆ Imagine that an area of park or countryside near your home is going to be destroyed to build a new road. Write a letter to a newspaper, either trying to persuade readers that this is a good idea, or trying to persuade them that it is a bad idea.

Before you start, though, look at the following list of techniques, that writers use to make texts persuasive. They are explained in *Chapter 8.*

- ◆ Assertion
- ◆ Emotive language, to arouse the reader's feelings
- ◆ Facts, to support an argument
- ◆ Features of layout and presentation
- ◆ Opinions, including those that claim to be 'expert'
- ◆ Persuasive language
- ◆ Repetition, to emphasise ideas and points
- ◆ Rhetorical questions
- ◆ Slogans
- ◆ A strong voice

Think carefully about how you could use them in your own writing.

When you have finished, look back at what you have written and see how many of the techniques you have used. How effective are they? How well have you fitted your writing to your audience?

It is worth having this list of techniques in your mind as a sort of checklist for the exam.

Writing instructions

The words in the box below are all useful for connecting or starting
sentences when you are writing instructions:

Getting started	You will need... Before you start... First of all...
Instructions	You should... You could... In order to... So that...
Making the order clear	First(ly)... Secondly..., etc Next... Now... Having... Immediately... Afterwards... Meanwhile... Whenever... When you have... Eventually... Finally...
Emphasising particular instructions	It is important to... It is essential that... ...more important... ...especially... Above all... Remember... Don't forget... Of course... Take care that... Make sure that... Always...

Try one of the following tasks, writing no more than 200 words. (This is less than you should write in the exam.)

Either

◆ Write about an interest or hobby as though you were explaining it to someone who is an absolute beginner, but is interested in learning about it and sharing your knowledge.

Or

◆ Imagine that the headteacher has agreed to build a brand new common room for Year 11. Give detailed instructions to the architect who is going to design the building, on what it should be like.

Before you start, think carefully about how you can lay the instructions out to make them as clear as possible.

As you write, use the list of words to help you.

When you have finished, look back over your instructions. How could they have been clearer?

Who would have thought that a simple phrase like 'pot-plants' could be so easily misunderstood...

Remember that the task you do in the exam may involve arguing, persuading and giving instructions all at once.

4 Writing to inform, explain or describe

In **Section B of English Paper 2**, you will have to produce a piece of writing. There will be a choice of three tasks, from which you will have to choose one. This will involve informing, explaining or describing, or a mixture of these.

Informing

means putting information across as clearly and understandably as possible.

"...she WHAT?!"

Explaining

means helping your readers to understand an idea or a point of view.

Describing

means putting across what something is like in an imaginative way.

After four hours she was confirmed as the world's worst charades player...

You will already have practised these kinds of writing in class. This chapter does not attempt to teach you how to do these kinds of writing, but it does offer:

- advice about how to tackle the exam

- some ideas as to what you should revise

- some suggestions for how you can do more preparation on your own.

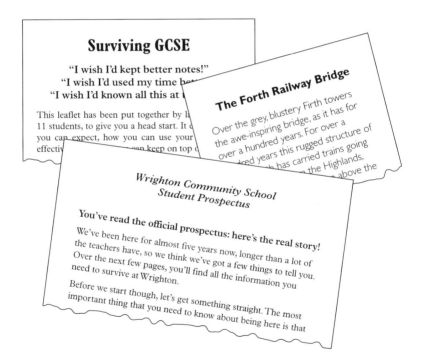

Surviving GCSE

"I wish I'd kept better notes!"
"I wish I'd used my time be...
"I wish I'd known all this at...

This leaflet has been put together by ...
11 students, to give you a head start. It ...
you can expect, how you can use your ...
effecti... ...een keep on top o...

The Forth Railway Bridge

Over the grey, blustery Firth towers
the awe-inspiring bridge, as it has for
over a hundred years. For over a
...red years this rugged structure of
...h has carried trains going
...the Highlands,
...above the

Wrighton Community School
Student Prospectus

You've read the official prospectus: here's the real story!

We've been here for almost five years now, longer than a lot of
the teachers have, so we think we've got a few things to tell you.
Over the next few pages, you'll find all the information you
need to survive at Wrighton.

Before we start though, let's get something straight. The most
important thing that you need to know about being here is that

What the examiners are looking for

✔ Can you communicate clearly in writing?

✔ Can you write for a particular audience?

✔ Can you use particular forms effectively?

✔ Can you use a wide vocabulary?

✔ Can you organise ideas into sentences, paragraphs and whole texts?

✔ How well can you spell?

✔ Can you punctuate accurately?

✔ Can you use standard English when appropriate?

✔ Can you present work neatly and clearly?

✔ How clear and readable is your handwriting?

Tackling the exam paper

Reading the paper

It is very important that you read all of the questions carefully before deciding which to answer. Remember that this section tests your skills as a writer. Think about the type, or types, of writing that each question asks for, and which ones you can do best. Which type of writing will give you the chance to do your best work?

In *Chapter 9*, there are examples of questions, together with advice.

Planning and writing

At the beginning of Section B there will be advice about how to spend the hour that is allowed for the question. You should spend ten minutes planning, 40 minutes writing and then ten minutes checking and correcting what you have written. It is essential that you use your time efficiently.

The examiners will be looking for evidence that you have put your ideas into order before starting to write. Make a list of points or a diagram of your ideas. Remember that you will be expected to write at least two sides in your answer. Careful planning is essential: don't just launch into the writing. Look at the example on page 37.

It is important that you think very carefully about the purpose of the piece of writing and the audience.

The most important thing here is to write something interesting, and to write in an imaginative or inventive way. Don't just string facts together: be personal – try to surprise, entertain, unsettle, intrigue or otherwise interest the reader. Find an inventive way of starting your piece of writing.

Whatever you write, don't do a rough draft – you won't have time.

Make sure that you write enough. The examiners will be looking for evidence that you can sustain a piece of writing (keep it going), so something very short won't do, however brilliantly it is written. Aim to write about two sides.

Real or imaginary?

A question might ask you to write about yourself – about an incident, a memory, or a place you know, for example. What you write about could be real or made up. You may feel more comfortable making something up, and you may be able to make it more interesting; on the other hand, people often write very well about real things, as they have more to say and have real feelings and thoughts to express.

Presentation

In some pieces of writing – a letter, for example – the way it is laid out or presented matters. However, you should not spend too long on this: the words are the most important thing.

Checking and correcting

Remember that this is one of the sections in the exam where you can gain or lose marks for spelling, punctuation, grammar and presentation.

Leave yourself time to check your answers at the end. Five minutes should be enough.

Practising planning and writing

One of the best ways to prepare for this part of the exam is to have a go at the kinds of questions that are in the paper. Ask your teacher for examples of these to practise with. Look at the advice on *Practising planning and writing* in *Chapter 1*.

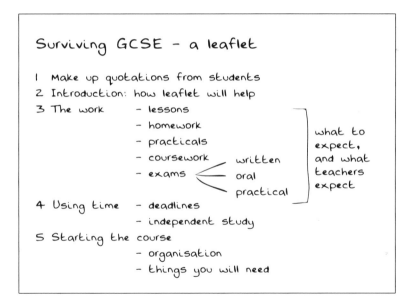

Surviving GCSE – a leaflet

1 Make up quotations from students
2 Introduction: how leaflet will help
3 The work   – lessons
                    – homework
                    – practicals
                    – coursework   written
                    – exams   <   oral   } what to expect, and what teachers expect
                                      practical
4 Using time   – deadlines
                   – independent study
5 Starting the course
                   – organisation
                   – things you will need

For this section of the exam, it can be particularly useful to practise writing the beginnings of texts which inform, explain or describe. How can you make an impact straightaway? How can you grab your reader's attention? Look at the examples on page 33.

Other ways to prepare for this section

 Choose one of the following sample questions:

Either

◆ Write an introduction to an unofficial school prospectus, informing new pupils at your school about what the school is really like.

Or

◆ You have been asked to write a short guide to starting GCSEs for next year's Year 10 students. Explain to them what GCSE work is like, how they can make the best use of their time, and how they can make a good start to the course.

Or

◆ Describe a place that you can remember well from when you were younger. For example, a house you lived in, a place you went to on holiday, or a place where you used to play when you were small. It could be real or imaginary.

 Pick one question and write down ten key words that you might use in your answer. Decide which three words from your list are the most important. Then decide which one word is most important. For example:

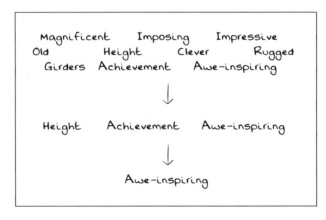

This sort of quick gathering of ideas and language can be very useful, and can give you confidence as you start to write.

Look back at your words. Can you replace any of them with more interesting words?

Girders ⟶ iron-strength

Clever ⟶ ingenious

Old ⟶ enduring

Now do this for the other two questions.

Look at your three lists. Are you choosing different sorts of words for the different sorts of task?

• • • • •

Look at the beginnings of some stories or novels – just the opening paragraphs. Which one do you think is the most effective? What has the writer done to grab your attention or interest? Look for examples of mystery, shock, surprise, strangeness, putting the reader in the middle of a story, and other techniques.

Now try using one of these methods to write the opening paragraph of a practice answer. Does it help you to get started?

It is important to make your opening as effective as you can. Never start in an obvious way: start in the middle, or with something that will puzzle or shock the reader.

Now he had the examiner's attention…

This is a good way of practising descriptive writing.

Imagine a place you know well, or an imaginary place. It could be any sort of place – beautiful, hostile, mysterious or ordinary. Get a picture of it in your mind and hold that picture for a few seconds.

Now quickly write down:

◆ three colours that you can see in the scene

◆ three shapes that you can see

◆ three textures that you can 'see' (eg 'spiky' or 'polished')

◆ three sounds that you can imagine in the scene

◆ three smells that you can imagine in the scene

◆ three feelings that you can sense in the scene ('gloom', 'joy' or 'anger')

◆ three metaphors to describe parts of the scene (for example, a tree might look like a crane, or a river might seem like a stream of blood).

Then try to write a description of the scene, weaving these ideas together. Experiment with mixing the different senses and feelings together, to create unusual descriptions: "spiky blue"; "dazzling bird-song"; "angry, orange light". Give yourself a time limit: it could be the full hour, or you could work for just 20 minutes, and see how much you can write.

Reread your description. How could you improve it?

●　●　●　●　●

This is a good way of practising explaining something. The words in the box on the next page are all useful words for connecting or starting sentences when you are explaining something.

First(ly)…	Equally…	In particular…
Secondly…	Similarly…	Above all…
…then…		Notably…
…and then…	In the same way…	Specifically…
…after(wards)…	As with…	…especially…
Meanwhile…		
Whenever…	However…	For example…
Eventually…	…but…	…such as…
Finally…	Nevertheless…	
	Alternatively…	Clearly…
Furthermore…	Despite this…	…of course…
Therefore…	…instead…	
Consequently…		…the following…
…because/as…		
Accordingly…		In brief…
…as long as…		On the whole…
		To sum up…

Choosing the right words like this can help you to suit your writing to your audience. Go through the list and pick out five words that would make an explanation sound more formal. For example, if you were writing to your headteacher you might write "Furthermore…", rather than "What's more…".

 Now try writing a short, formal letter (no more than 150 words) to a fast food restaurant. You are complaining that you found a human ear in your meal and you would like a refund. You need to explain what has happened and what you want to be done. In your letter, try to include formal words from the list. Remember to set your letter out correctly.

• • • • •

Note that the task you do in the exam may involve informing, explaining and describing all at once.

5 Revising a group of poems

In **Section B of the English Literature Paper**, you will have to write for an hour about a group of poems that you have studied. This will be from the NEAB *Anthology* or from another published collection of poems. As in Section A, this one essay counts for 35% of the total Literature mark.

You will also spend an hour writing about two other groups of poems for **Section A of English Paper 2**. These poems will be from the NEAB *Anthology*: a group of poems by one poet, and a collection of 'poems from other cultures and traditions'.

This chapter is about how to revise a group of poems:

◆ a group of poems linked by theme
  (English Literature, Section B)

◆ a group of poems by one poet
  (English Paper 2, Section A)

◆ 'poems from other cultures and traditions'
  (English Paper 2, Section A).

What the examiners are looking for

✔ Do you know the poems well?

✔ Do you understand how the writers have used language to create effects, and can you refer to particular examples?

✔ Can you say what you think poems mean or are about?

✔ Can you compare poems? This will usually mean comparing two, three or four poems.

✔ Can you show how comparing the poems has developed your understanding of each one?

✔ Can you make your personal response to the poems clear? This means showing that you have thought about them, and that you have ideas and reactions of your own; it might mean writing about what you liked or disliked about them, too.

✔ Can you show some understanding of social, cultural and historical context? (See page 50.)

Comparing the poems

One of the main things that the examiners are looking for in these sections of the exam is your ability to compare texts. You will be writing about two, three or four poems in each section, and you must show that you are aware of how they are similar (in the way they are written and in what they are saying) and how they are different.

You should plan carefully for this: the bullet points in the question may help you with this. For example:

	'In Tedium's Drought I Languish'	Sonnet 12	'Traffic Jam'
• Purpose	– Warning	– Seduction	– Announcement
• Type of wasted time	– Futility of a selfish life	– Lost opportunity in love	– Stuck in traffic
• Language and form	– Regular stanzas, rhythm and rhyme: monotonous! – Imagery of deserts and torture – Personification of time	– Sonnet form – Personal tone – Imagery of nature and death – Extended metaphors – Personification of time	– Simple, everyday language – Rhyming couplets – Irregular rhythm like the movement of the traffic – Personification of time

Tackling the exam paper

Reading the paper

Find the two questions that relate to the poems that you have studied. It is very important that you read both questions before you choose one to answer. Think about what you know, and don't dismiss a question too quickly. A question may look hard, but it may actually get you thinking in interesting ways. If you think carefully you may have a lot to write about it. You might immediately think that you have a good idea for one question, but are you sure you have enough to write a whole essay about it?

Chapter 9 offers examples of questions with advice on how to read them.

Planning

The examiners will be looking for evidence that you have organised your ideas before writing. Make a quick list of points or a diagram of your ideas: don't just start writing. Remember, though, that in **English Paper 2, Section A**, you only have half an hour to write about each set of poems, so your planning needs to be quick. (See the section on *Practising planning and writing*, page 52.)

Some questions were harder than others…

Referring back to the poems

You will, of course, have to look back at the poems before and as you write your answers – to help you to plan your answer, to find ideas and examples to refer to, and to choose words and phrases to quote.

The activities below will help you to practise finding things in the poems quickly, but you will need to know your way around them very well. Annotations will help, but do not just rely on these. (See *Annotating the text*, page 48.)

Technical terms

When you are writing about the poems, you should be able to show your knowledge of technical terms, such as alliteration, metaphor and so on. However, it is very important that you show your understanding of how the writer has used these techniques to create effects. Just spotting and listing them is not enough – in fact, it may lose you marks.

Checking and correcting

Leave yourself time to check your answers at the end. A few minutes should be enough. For example:

You can add extra bits in the margin, or at the end.

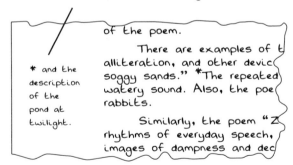

 # Beginning your revision

You can do the following for each of the groups of poems that you are revising.

♦ Reread the poems that you have studied.

♦ Look back over all the notes that you have made or been given when you studied the poems, and make sure that you understand them. You need to know about the main ideas in each poem.

♦ It is essential that you know how the poems can be compared and connected with each other. This is something that you will have worked on in class.

"I'm telling you the poems are connected..."

Annotating the text

It is very important that key ideas about the poems are at your fingertips in the exam. Mark key points and ideas. Underline useful quotations, or mark them in the margin. Concentrate on material to do with the main ideas or aspects of the poems that you have looked at. The process of doing the annotation is very good revision in itself.

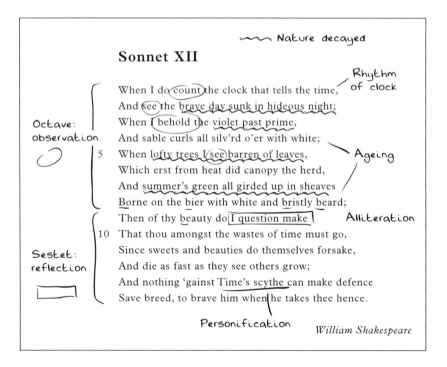

~~~ Nature decayed

Sonnet XII

Octave: observation

      When I do count the clock that tells the time, — Rhythm of clock
      And see the brave day sunk in hideous night;
      When I behold the violet past prime,
      And sable curls all silv'rd o'er with white;
5   When lofty trees I see barren of leaves, — Ageing
      Which erst from heat did canopy the herd,
      And summer's green all girded up in sheaves
      Borne on the bier with white and bristly beard;

Sestet: reflection

      Then of thy beauty do I question make — Alliteration
10 That thou amongst the wastes of time must go,
      Since sweets and beauties do themselves forsake,
      And die as fast as they see others grow;
      And nothing 'gainst Time's scythe can make defence
      Save breed, to brave him when he takes thee hence.

Personification

William Shakespeare

Do not forget the rules about annotation: you are not allowed to write more than one or two words at a time in the margin. Your teacher will be able to tell you whether you have annotated too much.

The examiners will know immediately if you are just copying annotations from your text. Doing this will not get you marks. Make sure that you are thinking about and answering the question, in your own words, and that you are getting across your response to the poems.

"Too much annotation?"

Social, historical and cultural context

One of the questions on the 'Poems from other cultures and traditions' is likely to be about the way poems reflect culture, and you should revise this carefully.

In the other groups of poems, the examiners will still be looking for evidence that you are aware of the time and place in which a poem was written, and about what mattered to people then or there.

If a poem was written some time ago:

◆ how does it reflect the way people thought at the time, or what they valued?

◆ how does it relate to the history of the time?

If a poem is from a particular country, or a particular culture, how is this reflected in the way it is written, or in its ideas?

You will have discussed this when you studied the poems and it is worth reminding yourself about it now.

You will not need to write about this at length in the exam, and not for every poem, but you should try to show that you are aware of it, even if that only means writing a sentence or two. The examiners will not be impressed by pages of background information – they want you to show what you know about the poems.

Quoting

When you are writing about the poems in the exam, it is important that you quote to support the points that you make in the essay. Well-chosen quotations show your knowledge of the poems. They also show that you understand the points that you are making. There are particular rules and conventions for quoting poetry. One of the most important is that you set out the lines as they are in the poem. For example:

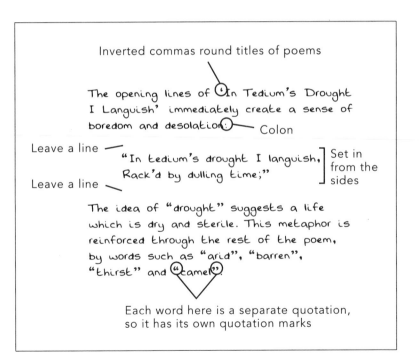

Quotations should be brief and should not dominate the essay. As a rough guide, they should not take up any more than about 15% of the essay. Never quote more than two or three lines. Usually, even this will be too much.

Practising planning and writing

To revise for these parts of the exam it is very helpful to get used to tackling the kinds of questions that are in the paper. Ask your teacher for examples of these to practise with. Look at the advice on *Practising planning and writing* in *Chapter 1*, and the example on page 44.

Other ways to revise a group of poems

You can do the following for each of the groups of poems that you are revising.

Thinking about the poems

These activities are designed to help you to find your way around the poems, to make connections between them, to practise selecting quotations, and to show you that you do know a lot about the poems as a group. Most of them can be done very quickly. Choose two or three activities to do in depth.

 Write down the titles of the poems that you are revising. Around each, make some notes on what the title relates to in the poem. What ideas does it bring to mind? What feelings does it suggest?

 Take one poem and try to sum up what it is about in five of your own words. Then sum it up in just one word. For example:

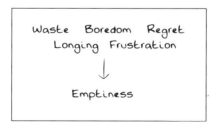

Try this for the other poems. Look at the words together. Are there any connections?

Five words came instantly to mind…

• • • • •

 Take one poem. Write down what you think is the most important line. Why did you choose this line?

Now pick out and write down what you think is the most important word in the line. Why did you choose it?

Do this for the other poems in the group. Look at the words together. Are there any connections?

• • • • •

 Take one poem, write down six key images (word pictures). Why did you choose these images?

Then select what you think is the most important image in the poem. What makes it important?

Now try this for the other poems. Is it easier for particular kinds of poem?

• • • • •

Pick one poem. Look at the first word. What does it tell you about the poem? Look at the last word. How does it leave the reader?

Then look at the first line and the last line. What is the effect of each?

Now do this for the other poems in the group.

• • • • •

Look again at the group of poems by one poet. Write down the first word of each poem. Look at these words together. Are there any patterns which might tell you something about the group of poems?

• • • • •

Pick a poem. Make a list of all the emotions that are in the poem. These might be in the experiences of any characters, in your own response to it, in the mind of the poet, or as suggested in the language in some way. Then write one or two words or phrases from the poem for each emotion. For example:

Anticipation < "dry mouthed" "tingling"

Excitement < "pulse racing" "fiery blue"

Contentment < "gentle waters lapped" "ease"

• • • • •

Do this for the other poems in the group. What connections are there between the lists?

• • • • •

Pick a theme that occurs in more than one of the poems in the group. It might be something like family, memory, childhood, nature, innocence and experience, environment, religion, community or difference.

Write down which poems relate to it.

Then choose and write down three or four quotations from each poem, that you might use if you were writing about this theme. Next to each quotation, you could write a few notes on how it relates to the theme.

What is different about the way the writers have dealt with this theme?

• • • • •

Pick three poems by the same poet. Make a list of similarities in the way they are written – in the use of language, the structure, the voice behind the poem, and so on. Then make a list of themes or ideas that you can find in all three poems, and a list of words or images that are in all three poems.

You will find that there is lots to connect the poems, but you also need to think about differences. Write down two things about each poem that make it different from the others.

Which poem do you prefer? Why?

After ten minutes he had picked plenty... but nothing he felt he could write about...

Writing about the poems

These activities will give you practice at writing in a concise and focused way about the group of poems.

• • • • •

Imagine that you have been asked to read out three poems from this group at an assembly for Year 9 pupils. The poems must be connected in some way.

Choose three poems and write a brief introduction to them (100 to 150 words), explaining what each one is about and what the connections are between them. What do you want your audience to listen out for particularly? What ideas or questions do the poems raise?

• • • • •

Take two or three poems that can be compared in an interesting way. Write between 150 and 200 words comparing the poems. You could write about the way the writers have used language, the ideas or themes in the poem, and your response to each one. Remember to write about things that are similar and things that are different.

• • • • •

This is a further activity for the 'Poems from other cultures and traditions'. You must think about the culture that is reflected in each poem. One of the questions will probably be about this, but, even if you answer the other question, you should try to refer to culture.

Take one poem. What can you tell about the culture that the poem shows or reflects? What can you tell about the way the poet relates to that culture? How does the poem draw on cultural experiences or knowledge that you are unfamiliar with? How else does the writing of the poem reflect a 'different' culture?

6 Revising a novel

In **Section A of the English Literature Paper**, you will have to write for an hour either about a novel that you have studied, or about the short stories in the NEAB *Anthology*. Remember that this one essay counts for 35% of the total Literature mark, which is more than all your Literature coursework put together, so it is worth putting considerable time into revising for it.

This chapter is about how to revise a novel.

*This was a tricky one...
reread the novel or go
out on the town?*

What the examiners are looking for

✔ Do you know the novel well?

✔ Do you understand how the writer has used language to create effects, and can you refer to particular examples?

✔ Can you say what you think the novel means or is about?

✔ Can you show your understanding of the characters?

✔ Can you express your personal response to the novel? This means showing that you have thought about it, and that you have ideas and reactions of your own; it might mean writing what you liked or disliked about it, too.

✔ Can you show some awareness of the social, cultural and historical context in which the novel is written or set?

Tackling the exam paper

See also *Chapter 9.*

Reading the paper

Find the two questions that relate to the novel that you have studied. It is very important that you read both questions before you choose one to answer. Think about what you know and don't dismiss a question too quickly. A question may look hard, but it may actually get you thinking in interesting ways. If you think carefully you may have a lot to write about it. You might immediately think that you have a good idea for one question, but do you have enough to write a whole essay about it?

In *Chapter 9* there are examples of questions, with advice on how to read them.

Planning

Organise your ideas before starting to write. You could make a list of points or a diagram of your ideas: never just begin writing. (See the section on *Practising planning and writing* in *Chapter 1.*)

He regretted now jumping in with both feet...

Referring to the text

You will, of course, have to look back at the text to help you to plan your answer, to find ideas and examples to refer to, and to choose words and phrases to quote. You will not have time to read pages word for word, and so you will need to be good at skimming and scanning. The section called *How to practise skimming and scanning the text* (page 64) will help you to do this.

Checking and correcting

Leave yourself time to check your answers at the end. Five minutes should be enough. For example:

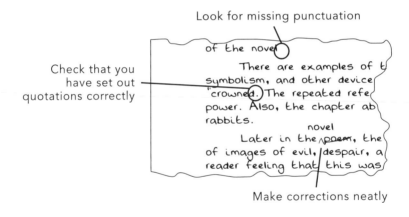

Look for missing punctuation

Check that you have set out quotations correctly

Make corrections neatly

Beginning your revision

Do reread the novel, if you can. It really is worth leaving time for yourself to do this.

You should at least reread important parts of the novel – key scenes and chapters. If you are not sure what these are, your teacher will give you some advice about this.

Remind yourself of the order of events in the novel. It might help to write a flow diagram, showing what happens, and which characters are involved.

Look back over all the notes that you have made or been given when you studied the novel, and make sure that you understand them. You need to know about the characters, and about the main ideas in the novel.

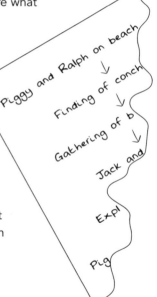

Piggy and Ralph on beach
↓
Finding of conch
↓
Gathering of b
↓
Jack and

Expl

Pig

Annotating
the text

It is very important that you do not spend too long in the exam looking for references in the book: know where they are! Mark key passages with a line in the margin. Underline useful quotations, or mark them in the margin so that you can find them easily. Concentrate on material to do with the main character(s) and with the main ideas or aspects of the novel that you have looked at. The process of doing this annotation is very good revision in itself.

Don't forget the rules about annotation: you are not allowed to write more than one or two words at a time in the margin. Your teacher will be able to tell you whether you have annotated too much.

Make sure that you use a pencil, not a pen, unless it is your own copy of the novel.

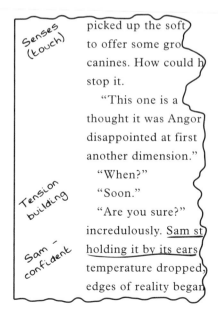

How to practise skimming and scanning the text

This is an essential skill for this part of the exam, so that you do not spend ages looking for quotations or examples to refer to. Of course, it is made much easier if you have annotated carefully.

Remember, this kind of reading is not about reading individual words, one after the other. It is about looking at large pieces of text, and quickly finding particular words or ideas in them. You should get used to looking at a whole page at a time. Try moving your eye quickly down the page, resting at three or four points, and looking for key words or phrases.

Most of the revision activities suggested later in this chapter involve this sort of searching in the text, but you could try this as well.

- ◆ Pick a character. Skim through one chapter looking for all the references to that character.
- ◆ Pick a theme. Skim through another chapter looking for the parts which relate to this theme.
- ◆ Skim through the whole novel, picking out any events, dialogue or descriptions that you think are important.

As you practise skimming, take this opportunity to put new annotations on the pages of the novel.

Social, historical and cultural context

One of the things that the examiners will be looking for is evidence that you are aware of the time and place in which the novel was written, and about what mattered to people then or there.

If the novel was written some time ago:

◆ how does it reflect the way people thought at the time, or what they valued?
◆ how does it relate to the history of the time?
◆ how does the way it is written, or the ideas in it, reflect the country or culture which it is from?

You will have discussed this when you studied the novel, and it is worth reminding yourself about it now.

You should not write about this at length in the exam, but do try to show that you are aware of it, even if that only means writing a brief paragraph or two. The examiners will not be impressed by pages of background information – they want you to show what you know about the text.

Quoting

It is essential that you quote from the text to support the points that you make in the essay. Well-chosen quotations show your knowledge of the text. They also show that you understand the point that you are making.

Quotations should be brief and should not dominate the essay. As a rough guide, they should not take up any more than about 15% of the essay. Never quote more than two or three lines. Usually, this will be too much. The kind of quotation that shows that you really know the text well, is when you weave quoted words into your own sentences. For example:

> From his first appearance, Jack is associated with death and evil. His "tall, thin and bony" body is skeletal – an image of death – and his "floating cloak" is reminiscent of a vampire – a personification of evil. His red hair is traditionally (and stereotypically) associated with impulsiveness and aggression, and his eyes are "ready to turn, to anger". (The "black cap", with its association with judges condemning prisoners to death, takes on a grim significance as the story unfolds.)

Practising planning and writing

One of the most important ways to revise for this part of the exam is to get used to tackling the kinds of questions that are in the paper. Ask your teacher for examples of these to practise with. Look at the advice on *Practising planning and writing* in *Chapter 1*.

Title underlined   Brief introductory paragraph

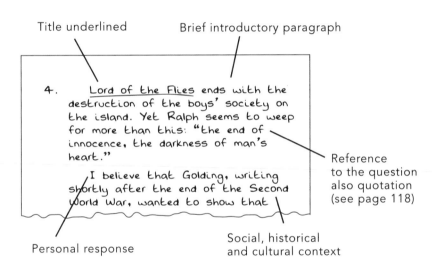

4.   <u>Lord of the Flies</u> ends with the destruction of the boys' society on the island. Yet Ralph seems to weep for more than this: "the end of innocence, the darkness of man's heart."

I believe that Golding, writing shortly after the end of the Second World War, wanted to show that

Reference to the question also quotation (see page 118)

Personal response

Social, historical and cultural context

Other ways to revise a novel

*Jenny was up in her room trying
out some novel revision...*

The following suggestions for revision activities are graded as easy, less easy and hard.

 Easy

 Make a list of the characters in the novel and write down a few words about each. You could also make a diagram showing how the characters relate to each other.

• • • • •

Imagine that a publisher has asked you to write a short description for the back of a new edition of the novel. It must be no more than 100 words long, and it must tell a reader what the novel is about without giving away the whole story. It must also give an idea of what kind of story it is, some information about the people in it, and why a reader might enjoy it. Try to sum up for the reader what important ideas they will find in the novel.

• • • • •

 Choose an important event in the novel. Imagine that you are one of the characters involved, and write between 60 and 70 words about what happened. To help you to get the most from your writing, think about these questions:

◆ why was it important?
◆ how were you involved?
◆ how did you feel about what happened?

• • • • •

 Pick one character and try to write for five minutes about that character:

◆ what can you remember about them?
◆ what do they do in the story?
◆ why are they important?

Then try this with other characters.

• • • • •

 Choose a theme or idea that you talked about when you read the book in class.

Write down at least three places in the novel where this idea is important. For each place, write down which characters are involved, and how what they say and do makes the idea clear.

Then find one key quotation from each place in the novel that you might use if you are writing about this idea in the exam. Try it for several ideas and give yourself just a few minutes for each.

 Less easy

 Choose a main character.

On a piece of paper, do a brainstorm around the character. You should include important scenes that they are involved in and themes or ideas in the novel that they represent. Note at least five quotations which you might use in an exam if you were writing about this character.

Write down how this character changes during the novel.

If you find this helpful, do it for more characters.

• • • • •

 Choose a theme or main idea in the novel. For example, it might be how people use the power they have, how people are changed by their experiences, or how they behave under pressure.

On a piece of paper, do a brainstorm around this idea. You should include scenes in which the idea is important, characters who show something about this idea, and at least five quotations which you might use in an exam if you were writing about it.

If you find this helpful, do it for more ideas.

• • • • •

 Choose an aspect of the writer's technique in the novel. For example, it might be the use of symbols, allegory, descriptions of places and characters, or a particular narrative voice.

On a piece of paper, do a brainstorm around this technique. You should include scenes in which this technique is clear, and at least five quotations which you might use in an exam if you were writing about it. Next to each quotation, explain why you chose it to illustrate the writer's technique.

If you find this helpful, do it for other aspects of the writer's technique.

•   •   •   •   •

If the chapters in your novel have headings, choose four or five of them. Make notes on how each heading relates to the themes and events in the chapter in particular, and in the novel in general. This will give you a useful summary of key points, and a helpful revision aid.

If you find this helpful, do it for every chapter.

•   •   •   •   •

Imagine you are one of the characters in the novel. Write as though you are reflecting on the events of the whole story. Looking back, what do you remember most clearly? How do you feel now about what happened? What have you learned – about yourself, about other characters, or about the world?

This will help you to revise the significance of your chosen character, and to explore events and ideas from an alternative perspective.

If you find this helpful, do it for more characters.

Hard

The first three activities are similar to the 'less easy' ones, but encourage you to explore more deeply on your own.

 Choose who you consider to be the main characters. For each one, make notes on the following things:

◆ how they relate to other characters.

◆ what you learn about them from this.

Look for three or four key quotations or examples to refer to in an exam. Does the character represent an idea or theme? Do they help you to understand an idea or theme in the novel?

Write down some key moments in the novel where this becomes clear, and then look for short quotations for each that you could use in an exam.

•   •   •   •   •

 Choose what you consider to be the main themes or ideas in the novel. They might include, for example, human nature, power relationships, racial tensions, conflict, history or the way that circumstances change behaviour.

Make notes on each idea. How is the idea developed through the novel? Pick out some key events which you would refer to if you were writing about this idea, and write down at least one short quotation from each. Are there particular characters who represent or illuminate the idea? How?

•   •   •   •   •

Choose what you consider to be the most important features of the writer's technique in the novel. For example, the use of symbolism, allegory, description of places and characters, a particular narrative voice, structural devices, or the use of particular kinds of language.

Write about where in the novel these features of technique are particularly significant, and consider how and why. Select appropriate quotations to support your points.

• • • • •

 Imagine that you are the writer of the novel that you have studied. You have just finished writing it and you want it to be published. Write a letter to send to publishers, persuading them that your book is a good investment for them.

You will need to explain:

- ◆ what kind of book it is
- ◆ what kind of audience it is written for
- ◆ what the main themes are
- ◆ main features of the plot
- ◆ techniques you have used in writing the novel
- ◆ why they will appeal to the target audience
- ◆ why you think your novel is important.

Make sure that the letter is long enough to communicate your main points, but brief enough to be interesting.

This is an excellent way of consolidating your knowledge of the novel, and helps you to become used to writing about it as a whole.

• • • • •

 Do some research on the writer of your novel. You might be able to find articles or books about him or her in a library, which will give you new ideas or perspectives on the novel.

7 Revising short stories

In **Section A of the English Literature Paper**, you will have to write for
an hour either about a novel or about a collection of short stories that
you have studied. Remember that this one essay counts for 35% of the
total Literature mark, which is more than all your English Literature
coursework put together, so it is worth putting considerable time into
revising for it.

This chapter is about how to revise the short stories.

*"Enough of the TALL stories... now
where's your SHORT story?"*

What the examiners are looking for

✔ Do you know the short stories well?

✔ Do you understand how the writers have used language to create effects, and can you refer to particular examples?

✔ Can you say what you think the stories mean or are about?

✔ Can you show your understanding of the characters?

✔ Can you express your personal response to the stories? This means showing that you have thought about them, and that you have ideas and reactions of your own; it might mean writing what you liked or disliked about them, too.

✔ Can you show some awareness of the social, cultural and historical context in which each story is written or set?

✔ Can you compare stories? This will usually mean comparing two stories and showing how comparing the stories has developed your understanding of each one.

✔ Are you aware of what short stories are – their forms and features, and how writers use them to create particular effects?

Comparing the stories

One of the main things that the examiners are looking for in this section of the exam is the ability to compare the stories. You will be writing about two or three stories, and you must show that you are aware of how they are similar – in the way they are written and in what they are saying – and how they are different. For example:

	Jill in 'Lady of the Hummingbirds'	Jack in 'Notice to Quit'
What the characters learn about themselves	That she has a negative side	That he can be independent, and how important this is to him
Beliefs and attitudes of each character	Tolerant; kind; looks for good in people	To start with pessimistic and lacking in self-confidence, as revealed by his narrative
Structure of story	Long descriptions of Jill; sudden twist at the end	Starts in present; flash-backs to threat of eviction. First person narrative
Language	– Long, descriptive sentences – Lots of metaphor – Rich symbolism	– Informal, colloquial style – Dialect – Lots of dialogue

Tackling the exam paper

See also *Chapter 9.*

Reading the paper

Find the questions that relate to your short stories. It is very important that you read all three questions before you choose one to answer. Think about what you know and don't dismiss a question too quickly. A question may look hard, but it may actually get you thinking in interesting ways. If you think carefully, you may have a lot to write about it. You might immediately think that you have a good idea for one question, but do you have enough to write a whole essay about it?

Chapter 9 provides examples of questions, with advice.

Planning

The examiners will be looking for evidence that you have ordered your ideas before starting to write. Make a quick list of points or a diagram of your ideas: don't just launch into the writing. (See the section on *Practising planning and writing,* in *Chapter 1.*)

Referring to the text

You will, of course, have to look back at the stories before and as you write your answers:

◆ to help you to plan your answer

◆ to find ideas and examples to refer to

◆ to choose words and phrases to quote.

You will not have time to read pages word for word, and so you will need to be good at skimming and scanning. The section *How to practise skimming and scanning the text* (page 81) will help you to do this.

Checking and correcting

Leave yourself time to check your answers at the end. Five minutes should be enough. For example:

Look for missing punctuation

Check that you have set out quotations correctly

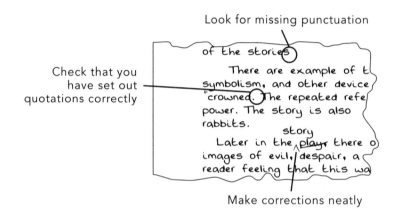

Make corrections neatly

Beginning your revision

Reread the stories that you have studied. It is essential that you leave time to do this.

Remind yourself of the order of events in each story. It might help to write a flow diagram, showing what happens, and the characters involved.

Look back over all the notes that you have made or been given when you studied the stories, and make sure that you understand them.

You need to know about the characters and about the main ideas in each story. To help with this, you should make a list of the characters in each story, and write down a few words about them. You could also make a diagram showing how the characters in each story relate to each other.

'Notice to Quit'
↓
Jack in bedsit, talking to friend, opening bott
↓
Flashback, through three weeks
↓
Arrival soon

It is essential that you know how the stories can be compared and connected with each other. For most of the revision activities that follow you need to choose two or three of the stories to work with. This is something that you will have worked on in class.

Annotating
the text

It is important that you do not spend too much time in the exam looking for references in the *Anthology*: know where they are! Mark key passages with a line in the margin. Underline useful quotations, or mark them in the margin so that you can find them easily. Concentrate on material to do with the main character(s), and with the main ideas or aspects of the stories that you have looked at. The process of doing this annotation is very good revision in itself.

Don't forget the rules about annotation: you are not allowed to write more than one or two words at a time in the margin. Your teacher will be able to tell you whether you have annotated too much.

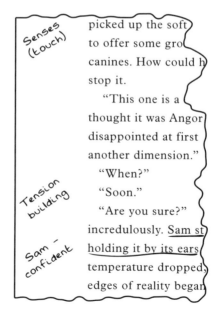

How to practise skimming and scanning the text

Skimming and scanning are essential skills for this part of the exam. Use them so that you do not spend too long looking for quotations or examples to refer to. Of course, it is made much easier if you have annotated carefully.

Remember, this kind of reading is not about reading individual words, one after the other. It is about looking at large pieces of text, and quickly finding particular words or ideas in them. You need to get used to looking at a whole page at a time. Try moving your eye quickly down the page, resting at three or four points, and looking for key words or phrases.

Most of the revision activities suggested in this chapter involve this sort of searching in the text, but you could try the one below as well.

♦ Take a story. Skim through it looking for all the references to a particular theme or idea.

♦ Then practise looking for moments in each story that you can remember and which might be useful. They might include a piece of dialogue, a description of a place or a person, or a significant event.

♦ Skim through each story, picking out any events, dialogue or descriptions that you think are important.

As you practise skimming, take this opportunity to put new annotations on the pages of the stories.

Social, historical and cultural context

It is important that you have some knowledge about the times and places in which your stories were written, and about what mattered to people then. You will have discussed this when you studied the stories, and it is worth reminding yourself about it now. You might also want to do some more finding out about it.

If the novel was written some time ago:

◆ how does it reflect the way people thought at the time, or what they valued?

◆ how does it relate to the history of the time?

◆ how does the way it is written, or the ideas in it, reflect the country or culture which it is from?

You should not write about this at length in the exam, but you should try to show that you are aware of it, which probably means writing only a short paragraph or two. The examiners will not be impressed by pages of background information – they want you to show what you know about the stories.

Quoting

When you are writing about the stories in the exam, it is important that you quote from the texts to support the points that you make in the essay. Well-chosen quotations show your knowledge of the texts. They also show that you understand the points that you are making.

Quotations should be brief and should not dominate the essay. As a rough guide, they should not take up any more than about 15% of the essay. Never quote more than two or three lines. Usually, this will be too much. The kind of quotation that shows that you really know the text well is when you weave quoted words into your own sentences. For example:

> From her first appearance, Jill is associated with life and goodness. Her "open, kind" face is "glowing" with vitality, and her "silvery, breeze-blown cape" is reminiscent of the wings of an angel – a personification of goodness. Her fair hair is traditionally (and stereotypically) associated with purity and innocence, and her eyes are "gentle and ready to forgive".

Practising planning and writing

One of the most important ways to revise for this part of the exam is to get used to tackling the kinds of questions that are in the paper. Ask your teacher for examples of these to work on. Look at the advice on *Practising planning and writing* in *Chapter 1*. There is an example plan on page 76.

Titles of stories in inverted commas

Brief introductory paragraph

1.   In both 'Lady of the Hummingbirds' and 'Notice to Quit', the main characters are put into difficult or dangerous situations. Both characters emerge from the experiences with new knowledge about themselves and others.

The use of flashbacks in 'Notice to Quit' emphasises the contrast between Jack as he was before the attempted eviction, and how he is at the beginning of the narrative. Jill, on the other hand, is

Reference to the question (see page 119)

Comparison between stories

Other ways to revise the stories

The following suggestions for revision activities are graded as easy, less easy and hard.

Easy

Choose a main character from one of the stories. Write down how this character changes during the story, or what the character learns. Write down at least three quotations that you could use if you were writing about the character in the exam.

Then do this for the main characters from at least two other stories. The ways in which characters develop or learn is often an important idea in short stories.

Choose an important event in one of the stories. Imagine that you are one of the characters involved, and write between 60 and 70 words about what happened. To help you to get the most from your writing, think about these questions:

◆ why was it important?
◆ how were you involved?
◆ how did you feel about what happened?

If you find this useful, do the same for one or two of the other stories.

Choose a theme or idea that can be found in more than one story. Find one key quotation from each story, that you might use if you are writing about this idea in the exam. This will give you confidence that you do have things to write.

Try it for two or three other ideas, and give yourself just a few minutes for each.

• • • • •

 Imagine that you have been asked to choose two stories to be read aloud on the radio. They should be connected in some way. Write a short introduction (about 100 words) to be read out before the stories, explaining to the listeners why the stories fit together. Be careful not to give away the endings.

 Less easy

 Imagine you are a character in one of the stories. Write as though you are reflecting on the events of the whole story. Looking back, what do you remember most clearly? How do you feel now about what happened? What have you learned – about yourself, about other characters, or about the world?

This will help you to revise the significance of your chosen character, and to explore events and ideas from an alternative perspective. If you find this helpful, do it for characters from other stories.

• • • • •

 Look at the titles of the stories. For each one, write some notes on how the title relates to the themes and events in the story. This should help you to think about what is important in the story.

• • • • •

Choose one story and think about a technique that the writer has used. For example, it might be the use of symbols, allegory, descriptions of places and characters, or a particular narrative voice.

Write down at least five quotations which you might use in an exam if you were writing about it. Next to each quotation, explain why you chose it to illustrate the writer's technique.

You could try doing this for other techniques in the same story, or for other stories.

 Look at the ending of each story that you are revising, and think about the following things:

- ◆ how did you feel when you got to the end of the story? Why?
- ◆ was the ending what you had been led to expect, or was it different?
- ◆ how did the writer lead up to the ending?
- ◆ what do you think the writer wanted you to think or feel at the end?

Make some notes on these ideas.

You could then choose two stories. Write about 150 words, comparing the two endings.

 Hard

 Choose two characters, from different stories, who can be compared in some way. Make notes on the following things:

- ◆ how do they relate to other characters?
- ◆ what do you learn about them from this?
- ◆ does each character represent an idea or theme?
- ◆ do they help you to understand an idea or theme in the story?

Write down some key moments in the story where this becomes clear, and then look for short quotations for each that you could use in an exam. How does each character change or develop in the story? What do you think connects the characters?

• • • • •

Choose a theme or idea which can be found in more than one story. For example, it might be human nature, appearance and reality, power relationships, racial tensions, conflict, history or the way that circumstances change behaviour.

How is the idea developed in each story? Are there particular characters who represent or illuminate the idea? How? What similarities or differences are there in the way that the stories treat the idea?

• • • • •

In one story, choose what you consider to be the most important features of the writer's technique. For example, the use of symbolism, allegory, description of places and characters, a particular narrative voice, structural devices, or the use of particular kinds of language.

Note down how the writer has used these techniques and why. Select appropriate quotations to support your points.

• • • • •

Imagine that you are a film maker. You are asked to choose two of the *Anthology* stories to film for television. The stories should have themes, ideas or situations in common. Write a letter explaining why the stories you have chosen would work well together and why they would be suitable for filming.

This will help you to think about connections between stories. Considering how the stories might be filmed is a very good way of thinking about their structures, their moods and what is most important in them.

8 Words to revise

When you are writing about a text – whether it is a poem, a novel, a short story, a newspaper article, a leaflet or any other piece of writing – there are special, technical words that you may need to use. Here is a checklist of some of them:

- ☐ Accent
- ☐ Adjective
- ☐ Adverb
- ☐ Allegory
- ☐ Alliteration
- ☐ Ambiguity
- ☐ Anthropomorphism
- ☐ Archaic
- ☐ Assertion
- ☐ Assonance

- ☐ Audience
- ☐ Bathos
- ☐ Bullet points
- ☐ Colloquialism
- ☐ Consonants
- ☐ Couplet
- ☐ Dialect
- ☐ Diction
- ☐ Emotive language
- ☐ Fable

*"There are all **SORTS** of words in here..." he shrieked*

☐ Fact

☐ Foot

☐ Genre

☐ Headline

☐ Iambic pentameter

☐ Icon

☐ Imagery

☐ Layout

☐ Logo

☐ Metaphor

☐ Metre

☐ Microcosm

☐ Mood

☐ Myth

☐ Narrative

☐ Narrator

☐ Noun

☐ Octave

☐ Onomatopoeia

☐ Opinion

☐ Pace

☐ Personification

☐ Persuasive language

☐ Phonetic spelling

☐ Plot

☐ Point of view/viewpoint

☐ Pronoun

☐ Puns

☐ Received pronunciation

☐ Register

☐ Rhetorical question

☐ Rhythm

☐ Sestet

☐ Sibilance

☐ Simile

☐ Slang

☐ Sonnet

☐ Standard English

☐ Stanza

☐ Stereotype

☐ Structure

☐ Syllable

☐ Symbol

☐ Theme

☐ Tone

☐ Trochaic tetrameter

☐ Verb

☐ Voice

☐ Vowels

Below is a list of words or phrases that you might need to revise, with brief reminders of what they mean.

Accent

This is the way that people from particular places pronounce words.

It is often important to people's sense of identity, and there is still a lot of prejudice about accents. Look at how writers sometimes imitate accent in the way they write words down. What effect do you think this is meant to have? (See **Phonetic spelling** *and* **Received pronunciation***.)*

Adjective

An adjective is a word which describes a noun.

For example, "cold", "clever", "happy", "exciting"... .

Adverb

An adverb is a word which describes how something is done, and is usually put next to a **verb**.

For example, "quickly", "happily", "predictably", "softly"... .

Allegory

An allegory is a story which can be read on more than one level. The characters and events in an allegory always represent something more general than just themselves.

For example, the novel Lord of the Flies, *by William Golding, can be read just as a story about a group of boys on an island, or it can also be seen as a description of how people come into conflict with each other in the wider world. The animals in* Animal Farm, *by George Orwell, represent particular people in the political history of the Soviet Union. (See* **Fable***.)*

Alliteration

This is where words close to each other begin with the same letter. You will find it used quite often in newspaper headlines, in poetry, or in song lyrics.

When you find examples of alliteration, always think about its effects. Does it make the language more striking and easier to remember? ("Brown's Budget Beats Blues") Does it emphasise the rhythm of the words? ("Full fathom five thy father lies") Does it work like **Onomatopoeia**, *imitating the sound of what it describes? ("Sudden successive flights of bullets streak the silence")*

Ambiguity

If something is ambiguous, then it could mean more than one thing, such as the newspaper headline "Giant Waves Down Tunnel".

It might be possible to interpret a line or a word in a poem in more than one way. Sometimes this is deliberate. For example, "generous laughter" could mean that the laughter is kind and giving, or that it there is lots of it. Sexual double-entendre is an example of deliberate ambiguity. For example, in The Duchess of Malfi, *by John Webster, an intruder in the Duchess's bed chamber is described as having "a pistol in his great cod-piece".*

Anthropomorphism

This is when animals or objects are given human qualities or abilities, such as when animals in cartoons or children's stories talk, wear clothes, and behave like people.

In Animal Farm, *all of the animals are given human characteristics. They are able to speak, reason and organise themselves as humans do. Think about why writers use this device. What does it allow them to do? Look for examples of anthropomorphism in everyday life, in the way that people talk about animals, cars, belongings and so on. (See* **Personification**.)

Archaic

If language is archaic, then it is old-fashioned or not in use any more. For example, the word "perambulator" has been replaced by "pram".

Sometimes, modern writers will choose to use archaic language to create a particular association or feeling. How is the effect of the word "wireless" different from "radio"? To a modern reader, the language of older texts will often seem archaic:
    "Thou tricksy Puck!
    With antic toys so funnily bestuck"

Assertion

This is a statement which is not backed up with facts or information.

*For example, the statement "GCSE exams are obviously becoming easier" is an example of assertion. It is stated as though it must be true, and does not allow the reader to disagree. Look for examples in persuasive texts, and think about why they are there. (See **Opinion**.)*

Assonance

Assonance is where words close to each other contain the same vowel sounds: "With dying light the silent fall of night".

*Does it make the language easier to remember? Does it help to create a mood or feeling through the repeated sounds? Does it work like **Onomatopoeia**, imitating the sound of what it describes?*

Audience

The audience are the people who read a text or listen to what is being said. The people who buy a particular newspaper, for example.

When you are talking or writing about a text, think about the audience that it is intended for: Who are they? How is the form and language suitable for this audience? What does the writer assume about the audience? What does the text demand from the audience?

When you are writing or speaking, you have to keep your audience in mind. Is the language and form that you have chosen appropriate? How do you want your audience to think, feel or react?

Bathos

When a writer appears to be building up to something, then deliberately ends in an anticlimax, he/she is using bathos.

This is almost always comic:

"Punark the Sorcerer was held in awe throughout the dark lands for his terrible powers of destruction, his unrivalled mastery of the ways of magic, his ferocious hatred for humankind, and his excellent recipe for lasagne."

Bullet points

- These are bulleted points.
- *They are used to make ideas clearer on the page, by separating them out, with a dot at the start of each one.*
- *Look at how they are used in informative and persuasive texts, where the ideas have to be as clear as possible.*

Colloquialism

A colloquial expression is one that people use in everyday speech, but not in more formal writing.

*For example, "bloke" is a colloquial word for "man", and "getting stuck in" is a colloquial phrase for "starting". Look at how writers use them to create an informal mood, or to give a natural voice to a poem, for example. (See **Register** and **Slang**.)*

Consonants

These are the letters that are not vowels (see **Vowels**), like B, C, D and so on. (*See **Alliteration**.*)

Couplet

This is a pair of rhyming lines in a poem, such as the last two lines of Shakespeare's 18th Sonnet:

"So long as men can breathe or eyes can see,
So long lives this, and this gives life to thee."

Think about the particular effect of rhyming couplets, especially at the ends of poems or stanzas.

Dialect

People from different places or cultures often have different versions of the same language – with some different words, different expressions, and different ways of constructing sentences.

For example, in Yorkshire dialect, "frame thissen" means "get yourself organised". In Scotland, you might hear the sentence "That door is needing locked", which shows different sentence structure from Standard English.

Oral poetry (poetry which is passed on by word of mouth) will often be in dialect. For example, the ballad 'The Twa Corbies' is in Scots dialect, reflecting the speech of the place where it originated:

"As I was walking all alane
I heard twa corbies making a mane"

You should look for examples of how writers have used dialect forms and think about why they have done this.

*(This is not the same as **Accent**. See **Standard English** and **Phonetic spelling**.)*

Diction

In a text, diction refers to the kind of words a writer has chosen.

It can be useful to think about this if you are talking or writing about a text. You might write about how a writer has chosen a lot of colloquial words, or technical words, or words relating to nature, for example. If you wanted to say that there was a lot of old-fashioned language in a text, you might refer to the "archaic diction".

Emotive language

This is language which is used to make a reader or listener feel a particular emotion.

*Always think about the effects of emotive language. What emotions does the writer want to make the reader feel, and why? It is used a lot in persuasive texts, such as advertisements, but also look for it in places where you might not expect it: in newspaper reports, for example. How does the headline "Jail This Beast Now" above a report of a murder trial suggest the reader should feel? (See **Persuasive language**.)*

Fact

A fact is something that can be proved to be true.

Fable

A fable is a story with a moral message.

Traditionally, fables have often been stories about animals, written or told to teach children about how to behave towards others, such as Aesop's fables. The novel Animal Farm *is a complicated fable written for adults, with a warning about the dangers of power. (See **Allegory**.)*

Foot

*See **Metre**.*

Genre

A genre is a "type" or "kind" of text. (In French, "genre" means "type".)

For example, in stories and films there are genres such as science fiction, horror, war, romance, comedy, and so on. Newspaper reports, magazine articles, leaflets and advertisements are all examples of non-literary genres.

It is important to think about what texts in a particular genre have in common. The features that they share are called the conventions of the genre. These conventions might include particular types of language, layout, or content. In a story or film, they might include typical settings, characters, events, themes, or ways that a story can develop.

Headline

This is the heading for a newspaper article.

Think about what effects it is meant to have on the reader.

Iambic pentameter

*See **Metre**.*

Icon

An icon is a kind of **symbol**. A graphic icon is a small picture.

You will find examples in leaflets, on computer screens and Web pages, in magazines and other texts. They make it easy for a reader to find their way quickly around a text.

Imagery

Writers or speakers often create "pictures" which help the reader or listener to imagine something clearly.

*For example, "as flat as a millpond" is an image to describe unusually calm waters. **Metaphor**, **personification** and **simile** are types of imagery. Which of these does Wilfred Owen use in the line from 'Exposure':*

"the merciless iced east winds that knive us..."?

*(See **Metaphor**, **Personification**, **Simile**.)*

Layout

This is the way that words, pictures, graphics, paragraphs, lines of text, headings, subheadings and symbols are arranged on the page.

This can affect the way something is read, and the effect it has. Look at this especially when you are writing about and comparing leaflets, articles or other informative and persuasive texts.

Logo

This is a design which symbolises an organisation or company. You may find logos on advertisements or leaflets.

"Actually it says 'logo'…"

Metaphor

This is when something is described by saying it is something else.

When you are talking or writing about a metaphor, always think about its effect. For example, "A monster chewing at the beach" is a way of describing the frightening power and animal-like energy of the sea. Think about the effect you can create with metaphors in your own writing, too. Look for examples of metaphors in everyday speech. Remember that a metaphor is different from a simile, because it says that something actually is

"What are you like…?"

something else, not that it is like something else. An extended metaphor is where one metaphor leads on to others. For example, in the opening of Hard Times, by Charles Dickens, Mr Gradgrind's forehead is described as a "wall". It then makes sense to describe his head as a "warehouse" and his eyes as "cellarage".

Metre

In poetry, the syllables in each line are sometimes stressed in a regular pattern. This is called metre.

To show this pattern, it can be useful to mark where the stresses fall, with slashes for stressed syllables, and circles for unstressed ones, like this:

o   /   o   /   o   /   o   /   o   /

"He threw the snowball hard and hit his friend,

o   /   o   /   o   /   o   /   o   /

He did not know, or think, how fun might end."

Read this out loud a couple of times and listen to how the stresses in the lines emphasise particular words. Look for metre in poems, and look for how the rhythm can help to create a tone – cheery, or insistent, perhaps. Look for places where the rhythm suddenly changes: what is the effect?

Each pair of stressed and unstressed syllables is called a **foot**. An unstressed syllable followed by a stressed syllable (o /) is called an iamb. A stressed syllable followed by an unstressed syllable (/ o) is called a trochee. Different lengths of lines have different technical names. A line with five feet is called pentameter, one with four feet is called tetrameter, a line with three feet is called trimeter.

Two common types of metre, particularly in Shakespeare's verse, are iambic pentameter and trochaic tetrameter.

- **Iambic pentameter** has five iambic feet in each line, like the example above.

- **Trochaic tetrameter** has four trochaic feet in each line, like this:

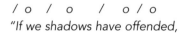

/ o   / o   / o / o

"If we shadows have offended,

```
/    o    /    o    / o    /    o
```
Think but this, and all is mended"

(See **Sonnet** and **Syllable**.)

Microcosm

In a story, a microcosm is a miniature version of the world.

For example, you might describe a school as a microcosm of society, with its own rules, leaders, ways of doing things, and so on. In the novel Lord of the Flies, *the island is a microcosm for the whole world: all the events and characters on the island represent aspects of the world as a whole.*

Mood

This is the atmosphere or the feeling that a piece of writing creates.

A poem might have an ominous, sinister mood, or it might have a restless, yearning mood, for example. Look at how writers use language to create particular moods.

Myth

This is a story originally told to explain something, or to represent important truths.

For example, the story of the Garden of Eden can be read as the story of how all people are tempted into sin, and lose innocence.

Narrative

Narrative is the way a story is told in any text.

(See **Narrator** and **Structure**.)

Narrator

The narrator is the person telling a story.

A first person narrative is where the narrator describes their own experience: "I walked into the room...". The narrator is then a part of the story, and might tell the reader what he or she is thinking and feeling. A third person narrative is where the narrator describes what other people do. "She walked into the room...". The narrator can be outside the story, and can be distanced from what is happening.

Noun

A noun is a word which names something.

This might be a person, place, object, feeling, or idea. For example, "Paula", "London", "pen", "happiness", "education"... .

Octave

*See **Sonnet**.*

Onomatopoeia

An onomatopoeic word is one which sounds like what it describes.

"Crash", "whisper", "rustle", "squelch", "bleat" and "snip" are examples of onomatopoeic words.

These are used by writers to create atmosphere, or to make an experience seem real. Think about how you can use onomatopoeia in your own writing, too. And know how to spell it.

...what with all the distractions of the exam room he had forgotten what 'onomatopoeia' meant...

Opinion (implicit and explicit)

An opinion is something that one person believes, but which somebody else might not believe.

Explicit opinion is where somebody states their own view directly. For example, "I think young people are rude" is an explicit opinion. Implicit opinion is where the view is not stated directly, but it comes across anyway. For example, in "The young person was typically rude" the speaker's opinion of young people is implied by the word "typically". Look for these in persuasive texts, and make sure that you can tell the difference between facts and opinions.

Pace

A piece of writing can seem to move quickly or slowly as it is read. This is known as its pace.

Look at how the pace of each of these two sentences is created by:

- *long or short sentences and words*
- *repetition*
- *punctuation*
- *mood*
- *alliteration*
- *long or short vowel sounds*

"Stretching lazily in the sunshine, listening to the soft, slow sounds of summer lingering on the heavy air, she drifted languidly into sleep."

"Now. I have to move now. Quick! Quick! He's almost caught me! Running, almost tripping on the broken ground. Sharp stones under foot. Can't breathe, can't see! Where can I hide?"

Personification

This is where something inanimate (not alive) is written or spoken about as though it were alive. For example, in Wilfred Owen's poem 'Exposure', the weather is treated as a living enemy: "Dawn masses in the east her melancholy army."

Sometimes an idea or a quality is turned into a character. For example, you might decide that a character in a story is a "personification of goodness", or a "personification of bravery". In pictures, Death is traditionally personified as a hooded figure with a scythe. In Animal Farm, *each animal represents a particular aspect of human nature – greed, cunning, unthinking loyalty, and so on.*

"Okay... stop writing"

Persuasive language

This is language that is meant to make people agree with a particular idea, or to make them feel something.

Emotive language is an example. You will find it especially in advertisements, newspaper articles and leaflets. (See **Emotive language**.)

Phonetic spelling

This is a way of writing words to show how they are being spoken in a particular accent.

For example, in a novel the characters' speech might be written phonetically, as in this extract from The Mayor of Casterbridge, *by Thomas Hardy.*

"But no – it cannet be! It cannet! I want to see the warrld!"

In a poem, a writer might use phonetic spelling to 'write' in their own accent. You need to consider why they have done this. (See **Accent** *and* **Dialect**.)

Plot

In a story or a novel, this is the order of events – what happens, and when.

Point of view/viewpoint

In a story, we will usually be aware of one character's thoughts and feelings more than others'. This is the viewpoint.

This may be the person telling the story, or it may be another character if the narrator tells us what they see, hear, feel and think. The viewpoint may change during the story. It is worth thinking about viewpoint in poems as well as stories. From whose point of view are we seeing what happens? Whose mind do we get inside?

Pronoun

A pronoun is a word that is used instead of a noun.

Examples are "I", "you", "she", "he", "they", "him", "her", "it", "them", "his", "their", "her", "its".

Pun

A pun (or wordplay) is a word that could have more than one meaning.

It might be used in a poem: for example, in this stanza from 'London' by William Blake, the word "mark" means notice as well as a visible mark, drawing attention to both ideas.

"I wander thro' each charter'd street
Near where the charter'd Thames does flow,
And mark in every face I meet
Marks of weakness, marks of woe."

In newspaper headlines, puns are often used to amuse and engage the reader. In Romeo and Juliet, Mercutio's dying speech is filled with puns:

"Ask for me tomorrow and you will find me a grave man."

Received pronunciation

"RP" is an accent that isn't associated with any particular place.

It used to be known as "BBC" or "Queen's English". Some people still have a prejudice that it is superior to regional accents.

Register

Register is how formal or informal written text or spoken communication is.

For example, letters and conversations between friends will probably be in an informal register – chatty and full of slang.
A school report, or a meeting between a parent and a teacher, will be in a more formal register. (See **Colloquialism** *and* **Slang***.)*

Rhetorical question

Do you really need to be told what this is?

(It's a question which is supposed to have an obvious answer, and is

Apparently, "Do I look stupid?" had been a rhetorical question…

being used to make a point. Look at how they are used in persuasive texts, to encourage the reader to think in the same way as the writer.)

Rhythm

See **Metre**.

Sestet

See **Sonnet**.

Sibilance

The repetition of "s" sounds in writing or speech to create a hissing effect.

In these lines from the play Hamlet, Shakespeare uses sibilance to bring out Hamlet's disgust at his mother's behaviour:

"O, most wicked speed, to post
With such dexterity to incestuous sheets!"

Simile

This is when something is described by comparing it to something else. When you are writing about a simile, always think about its effect.

For example, "The crowd is like a swarm of wasps" describes how the crowd looks, sounds and moves. It also gives a feeling of danger. Think about the effect you can create with similes in your own writing, too.

A simile is different from a **metaphor**, because it says that something is like something else, not that it is something else.

Slang

Slang words are words used by a particular group, usually when they are talking informally.

For example, "bunking" is one slang word for truancy, and children in different places have lots of other words for it, too. It is used in informal speech and writing, and is left out of formal speech and writing. Look at how writers use slang to suggest mood or to create impact. (See **Colloquialism** and **Register**.)

Sonnet

This is a particular form of poem, in which there are 14 lines, a regular rhythm and a regular rhyme scheme. Sonnets usually have two parts: an eight-line first section, called the **octave**, and a six-line final section, called the **sestet**. They are usually written in **iambic pentameter**.

The sonnet is a form that has been written for hundreds of years, and which is strongly associated with love poetry. The prologue to Romeo and Juliet *is a sonnet. (See* **Metre***.)*

Standard English

This is a form of English that does not include slang or regional dialect.

It follows a set of conventions that some people call "correct" or "proper" English. You should avoid calling it these, as that suggests that there is something "wrong" with dialect or slang. Rather, standard English is "appropriate" in formal situations. Look for examples of where writers have not used standard English: why have they done this? (See **Dialect***,* **Register** *and* **Slang***.)*

Stanza

A stanza is a group of lines in a poem, usually following a regular and repeated pattern of rhythm and line length.

Stereotype

This is an unfair view of a group of people, which sees them as all the same.

For example, an adult stereotype of teenagers might be that they are rude, aggressive, noisy and selfish.

Amazingly, she turned out to be a stereotypist!

A teenager's stereotype of adults might be that they all live boring, sad and conventional lives. You might find stereotypical descriptions in articles and adverts – of women, of old people or of the police, for example.

Structure

This is the way that a text is ordered or shaped.

For example, it is how a story begins, develops and ends; it is the order of ideas in a leaflet; or it is the use of stanzas or verses in a poem. It is always useful to think about the structure when you are writing about a text of any sort.

Syllable

Syllables are the separate sounds that make up words. "Go" has one syllable. "Going" has two. "Inexplicable" has five.

When writers use lots of one-syllable (monosyllabic) words, this might help to create a hard, blunt or even angry tone, or a direct simplicity. When they use words with several syllables (polysyllabic), they can create a sense of sophistication, eloquence or technical complexity – like that.

Symbol

This is something that stands for something else.

For example, on a persuasive leaflet, a picture of a candle might be a symbol of hope. In a piece of writing, a flying bird might be symbol of freedom, or fire might come to symbolise aggression and conflict. A reader might find symbolism in something, even if the writer didn't consciously mean it to be there.

Theme

This is an idea or topic which is important in a text.

For example, a story might be about the theme of loneliness, growing up, human nature, or friendship. You should be aware of what these are in any literary text, such as a poem, story, play or novel.

Tone

Tone is like mood. Just as you can speak in an angry or sad tone of voice, a text can have a tone.

*For example, a poem might be reflective or despairing; an advert might be lively or serious; a poster might be angry or accusing. This tone will mainly be created by the choice of words, but lots of other things create tone too – the length of sentences, imagery – even the layout and appearance of the page. (See **Voice**.)*

Trochaic tetrameter

*See **Metre**.*

Verb

A verb is a word which describes an action, such as *"build"*, *"destroy"*, *"grow"*, *"think"*, *"say"*... .

Voice

This is a bit like **tone**. If you imagine the writer speaking a text to you, the voice is the tone you imagine them using – the personality behind the text. *(See **Tone**.)*

Vowels

These are the open sounding letters in the alphabet – A, E, I, O and U. There are other vowel sounds, like OO or OW. *(See **Assonance**.)*

Additional words

Use this page to add other technical words you have used when writing or talking about texts.

Word	Meaning

9 Reading exam questions

In this chapter, there are examples of the types of questions you might find in each section of the English and English Literature exam papers. The way that the questions are asked or set out changes, so these are only rough guides.

Students often drop pints by misreading the question…??

This is an example of a question on non-fiction materials of the type that you might find in **Section A of English Paper 1**, based on the reading materials that come with the paper.

Section A: Reading

- Read Item 1, the leaflet *Your child's GCSEs: The facts*, and Item 2, the newspaper article *Exam stress: who needs it?* Answer **all parts** of the question.

  In other words you have no choices

- Spend about one hour on this Section.

1 (a) Read Item 1, the leaflet *Your child's GCSEs: The facts*

  According to this leaflet:

  (i) List four changes there have been in GCSE exams since they were introduced in 1988.

  (ii) What advice are parents given about how best to help their children to prepare for their GCSE exams?   *(15)*

Try to put things in your own words

This should be in your own words, but keep it brief

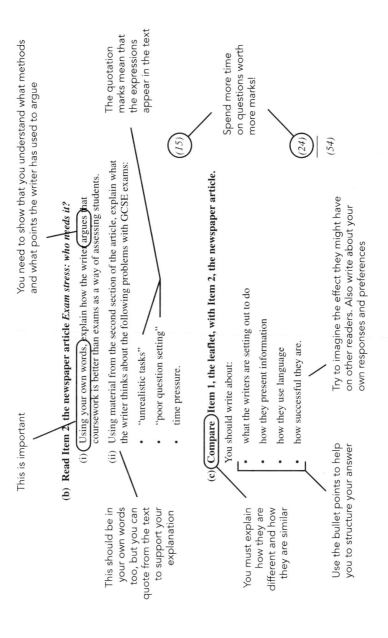

This is important

You need to show that you understand what methods and what points the writer has used to argue

(b) Read Item 2, the newspaper article *Exam stress: who needs it?*

(i) Using your own words, explain how the writer argues that coursework is better than exams as a way of assessing students.

(ii) Using material from the second section of the article, explain what the writer thinks about the following problems with GCSE exams:

- "unrealistic tasks"
- "poor question setting"
- time pressure.

The quotation marks mean that the expressions appear in the text

(15)

This should be in your own words too, but you can quote from the text to support your explanation

(c) Compare Item 1, the leaflet, with Item 2, the newspaper article.

You should write about:

- what the writers are setting out to do
- how they present information
- how they use language
- how successful they are.

Try to imagine the effect they might have on other readers. Also write about your own responses and preferences

You must explain how they are different and how they are similar

Use the bullet points to help you to structure your answer

Spend more time on questions worth more marks!

(24)

(54)

111

*This is an example of a question on writing to argue, persuade or instruct of the type that you might find in **Section B of English Paper 1**. The Section A which it follows contains text about blood sports.*

Section B: Writing to Argue, Persuade or Instruct

Answer **one** question from this Section.

Choose carefully

• You may use some of the information from Section A if you want to, but you do not have to do so. If you use any of the information, do not simply copy it.

This is important

• Spend about **one hour** on this Section.

Remember:

• spend 10 minutes planning and sequencing your material

This means putting your ideas or points in order

try to write at least two sides in your answer book

You may well write more, especially if you have large handwriting

• spend 10 minutes checking:
    • your paragraphing
    • your punctuation
    • your spelling.

Either

2 Write an article for a teenage magazine in which you **argue** either for blood sports to be made illegal or for blood sports to remain legal.

This is the key word

You should:

- outline what the law allows now
- explain your views on blood sports
- explain what changes you want to see in the law, if any.

This is the most important part

(54)

The audience is very important.
Your writing must be aimed at it

Summarise briefly

Or

3 A friend has been invited to take part in a hunt. He/she is not sure what to do.

Write a letter trying to **persuade** him/her either to take part or to refuse, depending on your view.

This is the key word

(54)

Or

4 A group of friends is getting together to organise a peaceful protest against a fox hunt. Write detailed **instructions** on how best to do this.

This is the key word

You should include:

- the sort of event that will work well
- how to plan the event
- how to avoid problems.

(54)

Use the bullet points to help you to organise your writing

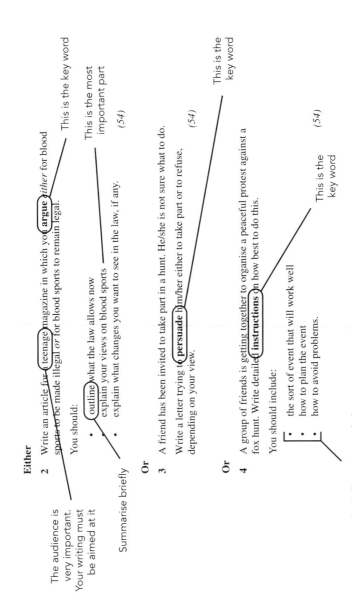

This is an example of a question on writing to inform, explain or describe of the type that you might find in Section B of English Paper 2.

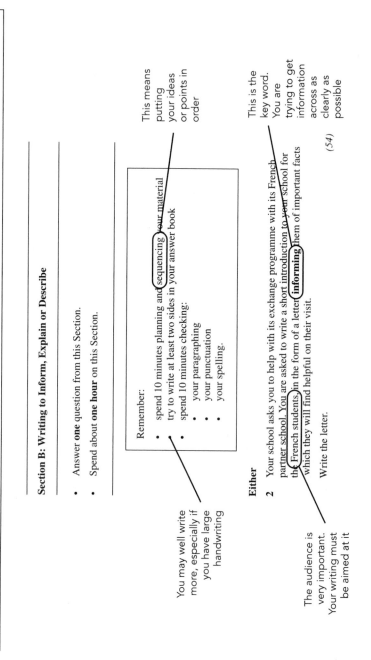

Section B: Writing to Inform, Explain or Describe

- Answer **one** question from this Section.
- Spend about **one hour** on this Section.

Remember:
- spend 10 minutes planning and sequencing your material
- try to write at least two sides in your answer book
- spend 10 minutes checking:
  - your paragraphing
  - your punctuation
  - your spelling.

This means putting your ideas or points in order

You may well write more, especially if you have large handwriting

Either

2   Your school asks you to help with its exchange programme with its French partner school. You are asked to write a short introduction to your school for the French students in the form of a letter, informing them of important facts which they will find helpful on their visit.

Write the letter.

(54)

This is the key word. You are trying to get information across as clearly as possible

The audience is very important. Your writing must be aimed at it

114

You are not just describing it.
You are helping your reader
to understand something

This gives you lots of freedom

Or

3 Write about a place that is important to you – it could be (real or imaginary.)

(Explain) what the place is like and (why) it is important to you.

(54)

This part of the
question is very
important

You are not just
getting information
across – you are
trying to create an
impression of
someone, in an
imaginative way

Or

4 (Describe a person you know well.) You should write about:

- what they look like
- their personality
- your relationship with them.

Even though it doesn't say
so, this could be a real or
imaginary person

(54)

You do **not** have to write about these separately.
You can weave them together. (For example, the
way you describe how they look will tell the
reader about their personality and your feelings
about them.)

115

This is an example of a question on a group of poems of the type that you might find in Section B of the English Literature Paper.

Wasted Time

In your answer to Questions 28 and 29, you must refer to **both** pre-twentieth century **and** twentieth century poetry.

The pre-twentieth century poems in *Wasted Time* are Sonnet XII: "When I do count the clock that tells the time" and "In Tedium's Drought I Languish".

You must write about at least one pre-twentieth century poem in this section

What is similar and what is different?

Either

28 We are all familiar with wasting time, and having our time wasted (Compare) how three or four of the poems in this group (present) the experience of wasted time.

You should write about:

- the poets (purposes) in writing the poems
- different kinds of wasted time (represented) in the poems
- similarities and differences between the poems
- the poets' choice of language and (form).

Instructions like this are very important

This means describe or give an impression of

What the poets seem to be saying, or the effects they are aiming for

"Represented" means put across through the choice of particular words and effects

Some questions will have bullets; some will not

"Form" is the way the poem is laid out on the page; patterns in the verses or stanzas or lines; the chosen rhythm and rhyme scheme, if any

*This is an example of a question on a novel of the type that you might find in **Section A of the English Literature Paper**. Even if you are not revising a novel, it will give you useful hints about how to read questions.*

Questions often use a quotation from the text as a starting point. This is designed to help you focus on a particular aspect or part of the text.

It is important to look for key words in the quotation to refer to in your answer

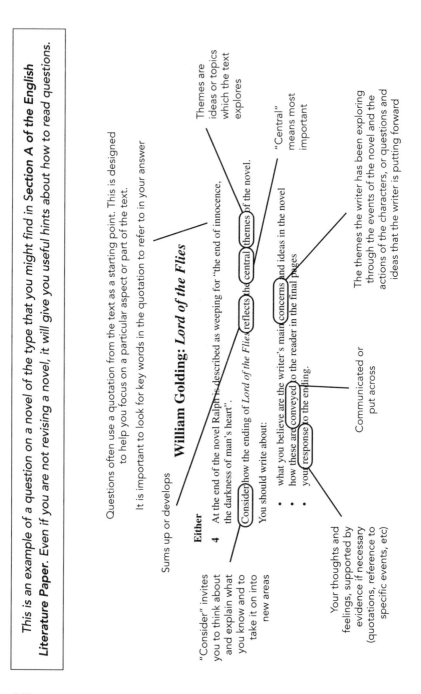

Sums up or develops

William Golding: *Lord of the Flies*

Either

4   At the end of the novel Ralph is described as weeping for "the end of innocence, the darkness of man's heart".

Consider how the ending of *Lord of the Flies* reflects the central themes of the novel.

You should write about:

- what you believe are the writer's main concerns and ideas in the novel
- how these are conveyed to the reader in the final pages
- your response to the ending.

Themes are ideas or topics which the text explores

"Central" means most important

The themes the writer has been exploring through the events of the novel and the actions of the characters, or questions and ideas that the writer is putting forward

Communicated or put across

"Consider" invites you to think about and explain what you know and to take it on into new areas

Your thoughts and feelings, supported by evidence if necessary (quotations, reference to specific events, etc)

This is an example of a question on short stories of the type that you might find in **Section A of the English Literature Paper.** Even if you are not revising short stories, it will give you useful hints about how to read questions.

NEAB Anthology

1   Jill in "Lady of the Hummingbirds" and Jack in "Notice to Quit" both learn something about their own lives. What do they learn, and how?

You should write about:

- what they learn about themselves
- the beliefs, attitudes and feelings of each character
- how each story is structured
- the effect of the language that the writers use.

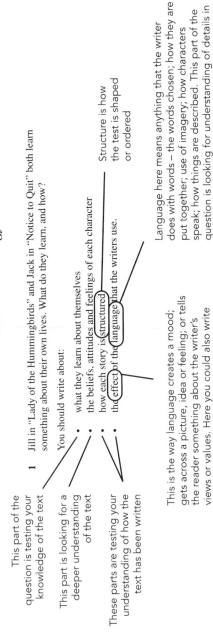

This part of the question is testing your knowledge of the text

This part is looking for a deeper understanding of the text

These parts are testing your understanding of how the text has been written

This is the way language creates a mood; gets across a picture, idea or feeling; or tells the reader something about the writer's views or values. Here you could also write about your personal response

Structure is how the test is shaped or ordered

Language here means anything that the writer does with words – the words chosen; how they are put together; use of imagery; how characters speak; how things are described. This part of the question is looking for understanding of details in the text

Notes